Dr Cherie Sutherland ___ ir-
rently a visiting researc ___ ṣy
at the University of N ___ on
near-death experiences and the author of the bestsellers
*Transformed by the Light* and *Children of the Light*. She
lives and writes on the north coast of New South Wales
and teaches throughout Australia.

# In the Company of Angels

## WELCOMING ANGELS INTO YOUR LIFE

CHERIE SUTHERLAND PhD

**Gateway**

Gateway
an imprint of
Gill & Macmillan Ltd
Hume Avenue
Park West
Dublin 12
with associated companies throughout the world
www.gillmacmillan.ie

First published in Australia and New Zealand in 2000 under the title,
IN THE COMPANY OF ANGELS, by Doubleday, Australia, an
imprint of Transworld Publishers Division of Random House Australia

First published by Gateway 2001
Copyright © Cherie Sutherland 2000
0 7171 3152 1

Printed by
ColourBooks Ltd, Dublin

A catalogue record is available for this book from the British Library.

3  5  4

# Dedication

*For Laif and Eden with love*

# *Acknowledgements*

Over the past few years my life has been filled with angels and I thank all of them for the blessing of their guidance and company.

A book is never written in a vacuum and the value of loving support given freely by friends and family can never be underestimated. I thank especially my parents, Thelma and William, and my two wonderful sons, Laif and Eden. I thank my very dear friends Maggie Hamilton, Peter Kingston, Alan Cartwright, Anthea Leonard and Kim Grey for their enthusiastic support, their open hearts and generosity of spirit. And I thank Rosie and Layla, whose diverting presence at my window so often drew me out of the clouds, out of my study and into the garden for long refreshing walks. Throwing balls and attempting against the odds to train puppies can be a very grounding occupation.

I thank all the people who told me of their angelic encounters—a happier interview experience would be hard to imagine. The many hours of our conversations have been transcribed and edited by me and it is their stories that form the sparkling threads that weave their way through the book.

And finally once again I thank the exceptional team at Random House, especially Maggie Hamilton, Head of Publicity, and Jody Lee, my angel of an editor.

# Contents

# Introduction

Over a period of seventeen months in 1943–44 in Budaliget, Hungary, four friends were regularly visited by angels. A month before the final visit, in October 1944, they recorded the following message.

Heaven descends.
We are the walls, you, the foundation.
If you are not at the mountain peak,
*Our feet step into emptiness*
And the new Home drifts.
The only error which your heart can commit . . .
Is to not be at the peak,
For then our feet step into emptiness.

My beloved ones, is it so difficult
To reach the mountain peak?
It is beneath the depths of the seas,
And it is far beyond the seas.
It is above, high above:
*In the depths of the heart.*[1]

Life is a journey of the heart. And whether we, in our more trusting moments head directly for the mountain peak, or at times of less certainty are afraid to leave the valley floor, we are never alone. The angels are always there awaiting our call. Seen or unseen, heard or unheard, these loving luminous beings are never more than a breath away, ever ready to shower us with their grace. But as they say, if we are not at the peak, their feet step into emptiness.

Almost always we must be willing to make the first move ourselves—angels are great respecters of our freedom to act and will generally not enter our lives unless invited. But learning to ask *from the heart* for guidance and help can be incredibly difficult in a culture which values success, self-sufficiency and control above all else. It can be terrifying having to *relinquish* control, admit that we need help, and then have to *trust* that help is really at hand. Unfortunately we are often brought to our knees before we even consider such trust to be an option. This is probably why many first experiences happen at times of physical, mental or spiritual crisis. At such times we are *compelled* to surrender and admit we cannot function on grit alone. And only then, at that moment of openness and vulnerability, do we allow their warmth to penetrate.

But there is an easier way. We could set off on this path before the crisis eventuates. Every day many of us block contact with angels by ceaseless noise, chatter and activity. One possible starting point for opening up this contact could be to set aside quiet time for prayer, meditation, contemplation, and other spiritual practices. When I look back at my own life it is clear that any major positive change has always come about after an extended period of stillness. This has happened so often that I now recognise stillness as a doorway through which angels love to step. What I have learned is that we need consciously to create a sacred space in our lives into which angels are welcomed. First contact may seem fleeting—a momentary flare in the darkness—but even the briefest experience of their light can fill us with rapture and hope, and give purpose and meaning to the dullest of lives.

The memory of such an experience can be inspirational at any time, and when life is difficult it can be a saving grace. We all have our ups and downs, even those who have been on a spiritual path for many years. Once when seeking angelic advice for a friend who had become depressed I was shown the image of a circle. I was told that my friend was in the centre, unaware of anything but the surrounding darkness of her confusion and despair, while just outside this dark sphere all was golden light. The message was clear: however alone she might have felt, she had not been abandoned. Even though she was unable to see beyond her gloom at that particular time, she was being reminded that the light was still there.

This vivid image brought to mind the opening scene in Plato's allegory of the cave. In *The Republic*, Plato invited us to imagine a dark subterranean world where prisoners spent their entire lives with their legs and necks shackled, facing the back wall of a cavern. A fire burned at some distance behind them so the only activity to be seen was the reflected shadow play on the wall in front of them. This dark world of shadows was their only reality.

Plato explored this image further by asking us to imagine that one of these prisoners was freed from his fetters and illusions, taken past the fire, out of the cave and into the sunlight. At first the man was afraid and could only make sense of this light in terms of the shadow play he'd been used to in the darkness of past experience. But after accustoming himself to the beauty of the new world he came to understand that the objects he saw were, in fact, more real than shadows and that this brilliant light was the ultimate source, even of shadows. And he began to appreciate that he was now seeing more truly than ever before.

In the final scene we are asked to imagine this man's predicament when forced back into the cave. No longer willing or able to function in the darkness, he became a fool in the eyes of his fellow prisoners. As Plato writes:

> They would say that his visit to the upper world had ruined his sight, and that the ascent was not worth even attempting. And if anyone tried to release them and lead them up, they would kill him.[2]

Unfortunately, among some sectors of our materialistic culture any suggestion of another realm peopled with luminous beings is, in a similar manner, likely to be greeted by howls of derision, if not quite by threats of murder. After all everyone knows that angels, those creatures of myth and religious tradition, have no place in a modern world. We are told that they are inventions—figments of an unsophisticated imagination—and anyone prepared to dispute the point is treated with disdain: 'How naïve!' Or, more angrily: 'How deluded!'

Our western societies are so proud of their rational skepticism and take great pleasure in exposing, ridiculing, and even annihilating any engagement with the non-rational. The suggestion that something could exist beyond the reach of our physical senses is roundly denounced as absurd. If it cannot be reproduced in a laboratory setting, submitted to scientific scrutiny, or analysed statistically then it obviously cannot exist. Or so the reasoning goes. And thus the material world is established as the only true measure of validity and sense.

But otherworldly phenomena, and even the little epiphanies of everyday life, have scant respect for such a limited view of reality. And we are all the richer for their intransigence. Of course our physical bodies exist in a physical world. But we, and this world, are so much more than just that physical manifestation, and to recognise this fact is to open the way to *en-spiriting* an otherwise literally dispirited reality.

Traditional societies have long recognised the presence of spirit in every thing and we would do well to reclaim that knowledge and become more aware, on a daily basis, of the numinous at the very heart of our existence. We need to rediscover wonder and reawaken a sensitivity to beauty. We need *consciously* to engage with the seasons, listen for the music of nature, taste the nectar, smell the perfume, feel the wind and sun on our skin, touch the earth, and feel the support of the sea. We need to honour the spiritual essence in all life and be grateful.

Even in an inner-city apartment we can practise an awareness of these things with simple acts such as lighting incense or a fragrant candle, giving thanks for a sun-filled room, for lavender and red roses, for the singing of birds, the tinkle of windchimes, for fresh herbs and ripe tomatoes, warm bread and homemade soup.

Rather than forever seeking meaning and significance in the material aspects of the world alone, we need to change our priorities, turn our attention within, and with renewed appreciation, reverence and gratitude, begin leading a more meaningful life. Of course striving and analysis have their place, but to routinely privilege them above contemplation and intuition can seriously impair our vision. Thomas Moore cautions:

> If we do not speak, think, and live in the language of enchantment, including naming angels and recognizing spirits, and above all, refusing to reduce experience to flat materialism, then the soul will go out of our lives and communities, and we will wonder why nothing seems to hold together and nothing is of absolute value any longer.[3]

If only we could set aside our Western arrogance and adopt an attitude of humility and reverence, the world would astonish us with its revelations. If only we could suspend disbelief and truly open our eyes and hearts, we would find that the universe is far more wondrous than we had ever imagined. And as this hidden world is slowly revealed to inner sight, we would come to know without a doubt that we are not alone, that we are always loved, always in the light, and in the company of angels.

# 1

# *What are Angels?*

A FEW YEARS AGO I was on a lecture tour when I received word from an American colleague that a friend of his, Jerome, had just been diagnosed with a particularly virulent cancer and had not long to live. As I was soon travelling to the city where Jerome lived I arranged with Margaret, my host there, to pay him a visit. As we picked our way through the clutter in the gloomy hospital corridor, she suddenly said, 'Oh, Cherie, I can see an angel walking behind you!'

I can still remember the look of amazement on Jerome's face when we appeared in his doorway. Although he did not see the angel who spent that afternoon in the room with us—and we said nothing about it—apparently he later told his wife he'd been visited by an angel. How often, I wonder, when we use the word 'angel' metaphorically, do we get closer to the truth than we realise? How often have we 'entertained angels without knowing it?'[1]

But what *are* angels? The term 'angel' generally refers generically to the entire heavenly host, as well as, more specifically to its lowest order. The very name 'angel' is derived from the Latin *angelus* or Greek *aggelos* meaning 'messenger' yet it alludes more to what angels *do* than to what they *are*. This is not entirely surprising since, as we shall find, angels, whatever their form, are usually so recognisable to us that we seldom stop to focus on what they are, being so swept up in what they are doing, and the message they are conveying.

And associated with these activities are their divine connections, for angels are not simply messengers in an everyday sense; they are messengers of God, intermediaries between humans and an invisible deity.

Carl Jung once commented that he was amazed most people so rarely turned their attention to numinous objects, let alone attempted to come to terms with them.[2] This is still true today, certainly in western society. But there have always been mystics and other visionaries who have described their first-hand experiences of the angelic kingdom, just as there have always been others equally positive that angels do not exist at all. It is the very numinosity of angels, Jung believed, that ensures arguments—whether for or against—are often emotional and difficult to ground intellectually. Yet throughout history there have been many great thinkers who have sought to make sense of this angelic realm.

St Augustine, whose life spanned the fourth and fifth centuries, believed angels to be composed uniquely of 'spiritual matter' and Moses ben Maimon (known as Maimonedes) the great medieval Jewish philosopher, believed that angels belonged to the realm of 'pure-form Intelligences'. A little later, in the thirteenth century, St Thomas Aquinas, himself often known as the Angelic Doctor, argued that spiritual creatures such as angels were in essence 'immaterial'. Immaterial they might well be when compared with humans, but on the celestial hierarchy descending from God, angels are in fact seen to be on the lowest rung, closest to humanity.

## The Hierarchy of Angels

Gustav Davidson, in his dictionary of angels outlines thirteen different celestial hierarchies attributable to authors widely separated in place and time. However, even a cursory glance reveals that these schemata share many similarities. For instance, most contain nine or ten levels of angels and, apart from the traditional Judaic and Islamic systems, share similar names.

The best known, and most influential ordering in the west is the *Celestial Hierarchies* outlined by Christian theologian Dionysius, an early sixth-century Syrian monk.[3] Strongly influenced by Neoplatonism and its devotion to the number three, Dionysius outlined a hierarchy of angels organised into nine (3 × 3) 'choirs'.

1. Seraphim
2. Cherubim     **First Triad**
3. Thrones

4. Dominions
5. Virtues     **Second Triad**
6. Powers

7. Principalities
8. Archangels          **Third Triad**
9. Angels

These choirs are usually represented as either descending from the Source as if on a ladder, or as moving outwards from the Source through a series of concentric spheres. However, whatever the spatial imagery, a distinction is always being made between the purity of spirit at one end of the spectrum and the grossness of the human world just beyond the other.

Dionysius writes in the *Celestial Hierarchies*[4] that hierarchy is 'a holy order and knowledge and activity which ... participates in the divine likeness'. The beauty of God, he writes, 'bestows its own light upon each according to his merit'.

Dionysius provides us with a hierarchy founded on the principle of levels of perfection—perfection being a measure of closeness to God. The highest-ranked choirs of angels are with God. They are able to directly contemplate the beauty of the supreme deity and are filled with the gift of divine light. Then, as 'bright and spotless mirrors', they reflect this light on to those further away from the Source—the level of light presumably diminishing as it descends (or moves outwards) through the ranks to the material world.

Within the Christian monastic tradition, St Bonaventure, a contemporary of Aquinas, envisaged this hierarchy as representing phases of the soul, and saw it as a means by which the souls of righteous humans could transcend matter and ascend to God. On the other hand, Meister Eckhardt, one of the earliest of the Rhineland mystics, envisaged the same hierarchy as a means by which God could descend into man.


According to Dionysius, the nine choirs are organised into three triads, each transcending and including all the qualities, illuminations and powers of those lower on the hierarchy. In the highest (perfecting) triad—the one closest to God— are Seraphim, Cherubim and Thrones.

The Seraphim—the 'glowing ones'—surround the throne of God and are often described as ceaselessly singing his glory. Dionysius explains that they purify those below by 'firing them to their own heat', thus dispelling the forces of darkness. The Cherubim—'the streams of wisdom'— according to Dionysius, are filled with 'divine wisdom' and bounteously pour out these illuminations onto those below. The third choir, the Thrones, he writes, 'dwell in the fullest power'. They are symbols of steadfastness and are forever open to receive the divine presence.

In the second (illuminating) triad are Dominions, Virtues and Powers. The Dominions, according to Dionysius, wholly give themselves to the source of true authority. The Virtues, he writes, are 'perfectly turned towards the source of virtue', and their role is to abundantly fill those below them with a virtue both vigorous and powerful. The Powers, he states, never debase their authority by use of tyrannical force, but rather lead those below them to the source of *all* power. They maintain order, and use the divine light to defeat negativity and evil wherever they find it.

In the third (purifying) triad are Principalities, Archangels and Angels. The Principalities, he writes, oversee nations, religions and world leaders. Just as individual humans have their own guardian angel, so too do nations.

With the choir of Archangels we reach more familiar ground. Three Archangels—Michael, Gabriel and Raphael—are mentioned by name in the Bible, and Archangel Uriel is mentioned in the Apocryphal Book of Esdras. Archangels seem to have a bridging role linking the higher levels of the celestial hierarchy with the lowest choir, Angels. And Angels, Dionysius writes, are 'the last of the celestial beings possessing the angelic nature' since they are directly in contact with the mundane world. The principal role of Angels, we are told, is to work directly with humans—healing, loving, guiding, inspiring and awakening us to our true potential.

## An angelic essence?

The relationship between humans and angels is a close, complex and fascinating one. In terms of *inner* connection, some believe we all have an angelic essence. Olivia, a fifty-seven-year-old woman I interviewed said:

> I think in the heart of most people there's a desire to
> believe in angels because we have an angelic centre
> within us that we recognise. Sometimes we try to be the
> best we can and that's our angel essence acting.

Emanuel Swedenborg, the eighteenth century Christian mystic and visionary, also believed that even while living in this world, in a body, a spiritual person might be deeply connected to the angels. He writes that in that state all thoughts, words and actions are inspired by this inner celestial connection.

According to another view, rather than having an angelic essence within, the character and behaviour of humans is seen to bring into the world particular types of angels. The Hasidim believed that kind deeds created kind angels and cruel deeds created evil angels. That is, they present us with a vision of kind people moving through life in a swirl of angelic beneficence and brutish people surrounded by a cloud of fierce and cruel angels. As Jewish scholar and rabbi, Morris Margolies, points out, Hasidic literature provides us with evidence that the function of angels, if not their actual existence, depends on the deeds of humans.[5] Similarly, in the teachings of White Eagle we find it said that 'negative or cruel thoughts ... swell the great streams of darkness' while 'thoughtfulness and kindness' contribute to the 'great stream of White Light'.[6]

It has even been said that human good deeds are needed to vitalise that greatest of angels, Metatron. I was recently fascinated to find reference to this in Guiley's *Encyclopedia of Angels* since one of my earliest angel experiences concerned Metatron, who said to me in a dream, 'I will give my life for you if you will give me life'. At the time I had no real understanding of what this message meant. I had never heard the name, and certainly knew nothing of his exalted position among the heavenly host. Margolies writes that in order for Metatron to continue mediating between humanity and the divine he needs to maintain his vitality. This is why he asks the 'righteous on earth' to generate enough spiritual energy for him to continue his task. If we refuse his call the consequences are dire indeed, for apparently if he is weakened, our hope of redemption through union with the divine is also lost.[7]

Swedenborg takes a slightly different tack. In *Arcana Coelestia*, written between 1749 and 1756, he states, 'The more we love what is good and what is true the more angels love to be with us'.[8] That is, while he does not exactly hold that we *create* angels by our deeds, he certainly believes we draw angels to us by right thought and action.

And for those of us with evil in mind? Swedenborg tells us that every person is accompanied not only by angels but also by evil spirits which actively inspire us to malevolence. He maintains that it is this balance of good and evil which keeps us in a state of equilibrium: always free to choose our own direction. In *Heaven and Hell* he makes it clear that the choice between good and evil is ours alone, but he does provide us, in *Arcana Coelestia*, with the reassuring news that angels *do* try to avert evil ends and replace them with good ones.

In western culture the divine origin of humans is generally long forgotten but wherever the divine presence is seen in angels it can trigger a profound remembering of our own angelic essence. Angels remind us that we are, and always have been, one with God. We are reminded of our oneness with all life and every animating force. And so importantly, we are reminded that separation from this higher force is an illusion. As White Eagle teaches us:

> Always, in your inner selves and in your quiet
> moments, you can rise into the perfect life, and

receive from those who dwell there the inspiration to live likewise on earth. Don't make the excuse that man is only human. With all the force of the truth that is in us, we say, we know, that man is divine.[9]

Even if we do sometimes feel ourselves to be but one isolated drop in an ocean, we are reminded that we are in reality a divinely animated part of the whole, connected spiritually to every other part. Indeed, according to Gnostic-Kabbalistic myths, before the Fall 'the whole of heaven was a single human being of fine material, the giant, androgynous, primordial Adam, who is now in every human being'.[10]

In 1993 a nine-year-old child, Erin, drew me a picture of the God she had seen during her near-death experience. It showed a figure which she insisted was neither male nor female and which had, as she said, 'billions and millions and trillions and billions and billions of heads—all the heads of the whole galaxy'.[11] At the time I was astonished, and still now I am amazed by this simple yet exceptionally perceptive representation of oneness.

A similarly vivid image, of a multitude surrounding the 'throne of God', comes from quite another source—Revelation 5:11 where it is written:

Then I looked, and I heard the voice of many angels surrounding the throne and the living creatures and the elders; they numbered myriads of myriads and thousands of thousands, singing with full voice ...

So what exactly are angels? Are they as most believe, a separate race of beings created by the divine, or could they be, as some suggest, simply the spirits of those who have died?

## Spirits of the dead?

In my research on near-death experiences over more than a decade, and more recently in my angel research, I have almost always found that people make a strong distinction between their first-hand experiences of angels and their encounters with spirits.

Perhaps the most easily discerned difference is between angels and ghosts. Diana, a forty-year-old woman who has had several unpleasant experiences with ghosts said:

> Ghosts are entities, spirits of people who've died but haven't gone to the light. They just stay on this earth not knowing where to go. I'm sure when I've seen them they're looking for help to evolve. But it's a frightening sort of feeling. These entities are always needy or wanting something . . . whereas angels are *giving*. And the angel I saw was so large! And the feeling was of total unconditional love. Totally unconditional love.

And Olivia said:

> Angel experiences are overwhelmingly loving. It's the love that shows it's the angels. You don't get love from spirits who are lost souls.

And Beth, with many years of experience as a medium, easily differentiated between her encounters with spirits who have passed over and the loving contact she has had with her guardian angel. She said:

> I get a completely different feeling. It's totally different to angelic. I suppose it's more earthy. Even though they've passed into spirit it's still more earthy. And the messages are more earthy-type messages. Often spirits will say things like, 'We've been at home with you and we've seen you reading books, and we've seen you crying, or we've seen you've got a vase of flowers' . . . These messages are just so the people can identify and know they have been there. Whereas with the angelic presence there wasn't that sort of message. It was an all-encompassing, loving message. And the energy was very different . . . To me it felt very different. I can feel it now. It gives me a feeling of . . . melting. It's an immersing . . . and whether I merge with the angelic energy or that energy merges with me, I'm not quite sure.

Of course when the spirit visiting is of someone close, the experience can be extremely warm and loving, yet people still do not confuse these visitations with those of angels. Moira, a woman who experienced a wonderful vision while praying for a friend she believed to be dying, said:

> It was just the most beautiful thing. She appeared to me. She was radiating light, looking at me, smiling and

nodding. It was wondrous . . . my whole room was full
of light.


(Unknown to Moira, her friend had died three days
earlier.) This spirit visit was undoubtedly very moving but
Moira still found it to be quite unlike her angel encounters.
She said:

> They are very different. With the angel experiences
> there's such a wonderful feeling of warmth and love
> and strength and power. The power is the wondrous
> thing. It's tremendous power. It's power that would
> overcome anything.


If people did speak of a deceased relative as an angel
their usage of the word generally tended to be metaphorical. For instance, one young woman said she felt her
deceased grandmother was now her 'guardian angel'. By
this she meant that she often felt the presence of her
grandmother's spirit with her, watching over and guiding
her *like an angel*. When I probed such cases, I found that
feeling the loving presence or even seeing a vision or
hearing the voice of a recently deceased relative was something frequently experienced, and appreciated, but believing that that person had actually *become* an angel after
death was something else again. As Craig Lundahl notes
in his article about the presence of angels in near-death
experiences (NDEs), the 'beings of light' seen by near-
death experiencers tended to be identified as either angel
*or* deceased relative; in no case was one synonymous with

the other even though their appearance could be quite similar.[12]

## Can humans become angels?

Is it ever possible for humans to become angels? Perhaps the most spectacular case is that of Metatron, otherwise known as the 'angel of the face', 'chancellor of heaven' and 'chief of the ministering angels', who we are told was once the very mortal patriarch Enoch. According to the Jewish mystical work the *Zohar*, Enoch was born with 'the divine spark of spiritual perfection'[13] originally bestowed on Adam. Once summoned to heaven, Enoch so impressed God that, in order to fully manifest his perfection, he was transformed into this mightiest of angelic beings described in so many tales.

God blessed Enoch with 1,365,000 blessings, increased his size until he was the tallest angel in heaven (according to the *Zohar*, 'equal to the breadth of the whole world'[14]), and gave him thirty-six pairs of wings and a countless number of eyes. 'Each eye was full of the glory of the Lord and each wing the size of the world'.[15] We are told that when invoked, Metatron could appear as 'a pillar of fire, his face more dazzling than the sun'[16] and he was thereafter said to reside in the seventh heaven, nearest the throne of God.

In addition, Metatron (as the Angel of the Lord) stands at the top of the Tree of Life and is often said to be the most significant intermediary between humanity and the divine. He is the chief recording angel, the scribe of heaven, recorder of all our deeds. And among his own many deeds he is said to have led the children of Israel through the wilderness, to have wrestled with Jacob and stopped

Abraham from sacrificing his son, Isaac. Despite his humble origin there can be no doubt that Metatron is one of the greatest of angels.[17]

On another level, St Augustine, the most influential of early Christian church fathers, taught that all good humans who tried to be like good angels, if successful, could actually become angels in the City of God. And, looking at it from the other side, Swedenborg believed that *all* angels and other spirit beings did begin life as humans. In *Divine Providence* he wrote unequivocally, 'No angels or spirits were created as such, but were born as people first.'[18]

If they were born as people first, how did they make the transition? Certainly not many of us could lay claim to Enoch's 'divine spark of spiritual perfection'. But there might yet be a place for us in the angelic kingdom ... perhaps more humbly as 'apprentice angels', our training beginning here on earth and continuing in the world of light after death. Perhaps there is even a sort of mentor system in which more experienced spiritual beings help us to find our wings and learn to fly.

In her wonderful book, *Commune with the Angels*, Jane Howard writes about 'The Angels of Earth', proposing 'human angels' as the tenth rank following on from the nine choirs of angels outlined by Dionysius. The key to becoming an earth angel, Howard tells us, is unselfish service to others.

Swedenborg believed that beginning life in human form gave us all the opportunity to exercise our divinely given free will, to make our own life choices and establish our own life patterns. This is undoubtedly true. These choices and patterns, which in simple terms come to define who we are, continue to exist in the after-death state where, according to Swedenborg, we awaken to find ourselves in a place somewhere between heaven and hell (these being states of mind rather than actual places). What then follows is a process of transformation during which we continue to learn and grow spiritually, some of us eventually truly becoming angels.

In Dionysius's celestial hierarchy there is no rank between angels and humans but in Maimonedes's schema there is an intermediate rank which are called Ishim. These angels, who are said to appear in prophetic visions, are believed to be the 'beautiful souls of just men'.[19]

For those of us still on the earthly plane, it can be pleasing to think that such closely allied angelic beings exist, since as role models they are aspects of the divine to whom it is fairly easy to relate. They feel familiar to us when compared with the awesomeness of some other manifestations of the heavenly host.

By identifying with the angelic essence within, by studying the qualities of angels, following their example and dedicating our lives to love and service, I believe it is indeed possible to become honorary angels here and now. Even though, in our outer world, we might be weighed down with matter and the material life, in our inner world, with angelic assistance we *can* learn to soar.

## Angels in human form?

Despite Maimonedes's strong assertion that angels can *never* appear in bodily form, there are nevertheless many accounts—ancient and modern—of their visits. For instance, Melvin Morse writes of a friend who, at a time of spiritual crisis, went hiking in the mountains. At one point, she called out to God for a sign, whereupon a woman dressed entirely in white came around a bend in the trail, walked up to her and addressed her by name. 'Go with God,' she said, and then went on her way.[20]

And Dylan, a retired scientist, feels it was an angel in human form who gave him the jolt he needed to face up to the fact that he was an alcoholic. His story illustrates well the impact even a brief angelic appearance can have on someone's life. He said:

This happened on 11 November 1977. At that time I was drinking a lot and had gone up the coast and spent some days up there drinking. On the Friday morning I decided to drive home but I couldn't find my way out of the town [laughs]—I wasn't entirely drunken but I was quite tipsy.

Soon after, driving along a country road, there was a little truck in front of me going rather slowly. I looked in my rear-view mirror—the only car I could see was about two hundred yards behind me—so I pulled out to pass this truck. But apparently the man behind me was coming along much faster than I expected because just as I pulled out he began passing me. We three were abreast for a short time and he banged into my right-hand side. In panic I stood on the accelerator instead of the brake, and shot through and passed the truck. I then pulled up and this man pulled up in front of me. This man who might have been a man.

When he got out of the car he was very calm and I remember he had a twinkle in his eye. We exchanged names and addresses—he said his name was Popov, which in Russian means Pope's son. We parted and I've

never heard from him since. My insurance company
tried to contact him but the address didn't exist.

I was quite shaken up by the experience but
I managed to get home without any further crashes.
There was quite a dent in the right-hand side but that
was the only trouble with my car. As soon as I got
home I had some more to drink. I drank all day
Saturday, and by Sunday there wasn't a drop left to
drink in the house so I went to my lab and filled an
empty gin bottle with industrial alcohol and came home
and drank it with orange juice. By that time I'd been
drinking for thirty-nine years. I vaguely remember
going to bed on the Sunday evening, and when I woke
up on the Monday morning it just hit me—I thought,
'Good God, I'm an alcoholic!' And I was very
surprised.

I'd never heard of detoxing, but by eleven o'clock
I was in a clinic and by five past eleven, a psychiatrist
there had diagnosed me as an alcoholic. An AA
member called that evening and took me to a meeting
and I haven't had a drink since. I haven't even wanted
to have a drink since. That was twenty-one years ago.

I feel that that bang on the side was a real wake-up
call to me. Half an inch either way and I would've been
killed. How I got out of it alive I don't know, except
that later it dawned on me that maybe Popov was an
angel. I certainly needed spiritual help from somewhere!

He was so calm and he had such a twinkle in his eye.
Either he was an angel or somebody sent by my Higher
Power. I'm sure he was sent just to wake me up. After
the accident he got in his car and was out of sight
before I could open my door.

In the Bible there are several episodes in which angels appear in human form. We are told that Abraham welcomed three strangers who materialised, in the heat of the day, at his tent by the oaks of Mamre. These three, disguised as men, were later revealed to be two angels and Yahweh Himself, who announced to Abraham that his aged wife, Sarah, would bear him a child.[21]

Similarly, two angels in human form were met by Lot at the gateway to Sodom, and agreed to accept his hospitality. Later that night Lot unhesitatingly defended his guests against the depredations of the population of Sodom who surrounded his house calling out for them. His reward for such righteousness was to be delivered (along with his wife and two daughters) to a place of safety before the entire cities of Sodom and Gomorrah were destroyed by a rain of 'sulphur and fire'.[22]

And Raphael, disguised as a young man, is said to have accompanied Tobias on a journey, guiding him safely to his destination and home again. In addition, during the journey he made known to Tobias the remedy needed to heal the blind eyes of his father Tobit. Soon after their return, Tobias applied the fish gall to his father's eyes and 'peeled off the white films'[23], whereupon Tobit regained his sight.

In 1990, a young brother and sister were travelling alone from Australia to America to meet their parents. Angela, the sister, who was eleven years old at the time felt they were being accompanied and protected by a man they met on the plane.

Sitting in the plane there was a man. He had white hair and he was just so nice. He was with a lady and he

kept talking to us. He was the most beautiful person
I can remember.

The plane had been delayed and was running
extremely late when we got into the airport at
Hawaii ... Mum and Dad were standing outside
waiting for us with hundreds of other people waiting
for everyone to come through. We hadn't told this man
what Mum and Dad looked like or anything about
them but he walked straight up to them and said, 'Your
children are very special people. You should be
commended on having such wonderful children. And
don't worry, they'll always be safe.' And he just went.

The weird thing is, after our trip, on our way home,
we were walking through the carpark at the airport and
my brother and I just felt ... We both turned around at
the same time and there's the same man walking a step
behind us through the carpark. He just waved to us and
then off he went.


Are these people really angels in human form or are they
normal human beings, who for a short time are being used
by angels for some divine purpose? Does it really matter?
The result is the same—the hand of the divine is reaching
into people's lives. An alcoholic is jolted into sobriety and
two children are safely chaperoned to the other side of the
world and home again. Indeed, even by reading such stories,
and (if we have our doubts) by wondering about such
events, we are ourselves engaging with the divine and angels
are reaching into *our* lives.

## Angels in nature

Every form of life—not only humankind—has a spiritual aspect and the natural kingdom is no different. Traditional societies throughout the world have always recognised this, working with and honouring the spiritual essence and guardian of each species and natural feature within their world.

My first experience of this realm occurred a few years ago. I was seeking an angelic message to pass on to my son, Eden, for his birthday. He had recently bought a farm and was living in a shed on the property while his house was being built. We had often walked over the land together, an eagle hovering overhead, while he familiarised himself with every dip and rise. We had also plunged into the rainforest on its western edge, finding our way under the dense canopy to what I always thought of as the grandfather tree—a lichen-covered giant with tall spreading buttress roots ready to embrace anyone who settled between them. We both knew it was a very special place so the form the message took should not have come as a great surprise.

During a visionary experience I was shown Eden's property filled with angelic presences—in every blade of grass, every vine, bush, tree, insect, bird and animal. He was told to be consciously aware of, and to appreciate, this sacred participation; to consult the angelic presence as he worked on the land and to express gratitude for their help. Then, just as I thought the message was coming to an end, I was amazed to see an awesomely huge angel overseeing the whole property, the energy streaming up from every inch of it to form a majestic body of light which reached up high above the trees to her beautiful shimmering head. This angel was no will-o'-the-wisp, but a substantial luminous form firmly anchoring energy over the entirety of Eden's hill. And then she said she was *very* pleased to have him there.

In the twentieth century, especially in western societies we have so abused the natural world in our desire to make it more productive that we have become alienated from these angels of nature whose powerful presence showers our crops, flower gardens, forests and wild areas with grace and light. Fortunately there is a dawning realisation in some quarters that the clear-felling of native forests, the destruction of natural habitats, the reclamation of wetlands, the spraying of chemicals, mining and genetic engineering not only damage the physical aspect of the natural environment, but also cause distress at a spiritual level.

Dorothy Maclean, best known as one of the founders of Findhorn—the spiritual community in the north of Scotland famous for its cooperation with nature spirits—writes in her autobiography of visiting a wilderness area in California where she found the *devas* in shock instead of in their usual joyous state.[24] The relentless encroachment of men and machines, thoughtlessly felling trees all around, was deeply felt by them and, as she suggests, perhaps they even foresaw that this terrible juggernaut would eventually move into their own wild valley.

What we seem to have forgotten is that *all* species are aspects of the One Great Spirit. So as we unbalance and destroy the natural world we inevitably unbalance and destroy ourselves. Poetic justice, some would say. Yet it is nothing short of tragedy that wholesale destruction has continued unabated, indeed with government *encouragement*, until recently, motivated by self-interest—our own survival—some humans have finally begun to explore the possibility that we might in fact be better served by managing our resources more responsibly.

I suppose it is a start, but unfortunately self-interest is never a sufficient motivating force for touching the deep heart of ecological problems and bringing about meaningful change. We need something more. We need to learn from the respect and reverence shown by traditional cultures towards their land and all its creatures. We desperately need to open our eyes, to see our world differently, to make an immense change in awareness and attitude. Perhaps then, if we show proper deference and a willingness to change, we will be helped to repair the terrible damage we have caused. Help *is* always at hand but we must be sincere in our desire to learn, and to cooperate with the angelic guides from this other—non-human—world.

We also need to understand that in angelic realms, in addition to those angels who occupy themselves with humans, there are other groups such as the *aqui* who oversee animals; the *elementals* who work with the four elements (earth, water, fire, air); and the *devas* who work with plants.

Within the grouping of *aqui* are the strangely named *budiels* who watch over the evolution of each animal species, and *folatels* who care for their physical wellbeing,[25] but probably those best known to us are the elementals. Through folklore we have all heard of gnomes, elves and fairies in the earth realm; water sprites or *undines* in the water realm, *salamanders* in the fire realm and *sylphs* in the realm of air. However these domains are far more complex than we might think.

For instance, the earth realm teems with a hierarchy of beings who, at the highest levels, range from the grandest 'Lord of the Mountain' to tree *devas* who, when sufficiently advanced, evolve into angels such as the one overseeing Eden's hill. These angels are described by Flower Newhouse as 'tall, glorious, beautiful beyond anything we know on earth'.[26]

Next, in descending order, come gnomes, elves and fairies and then the tiniest of earth elementals who tend the spirit essence of plants and minerals. These lively little creatures are described by Flower Newhouse as 'delightfully busy creatures [who] create a sea of luminescent activity across the landscape'.[27] And even at a microscopic level there are little nature spirits, minute angelic presences joyously engaged in the task of carrying vitality throughout all parts of a plant. And as White Eagle says:

Even the minerals are alive with the light of God. Each wayside stone is vibrating with a light and life it shares with every plant that grows. If you had clear vision, you would see that all the flowers and trees in your garden are pulsating, vibrating with colour and life . . . All nature is pulsating with this divine life.[28]

Ten years ago I heard an unforgettable story from Moira, whose experience of 'clear vision' perfectly illustrates the point White Eagle is making. She said:

I love nature and I have a great affinity with trees because my grandest, most wonderful experience was with trees . . . I'd been very ill and going through a lot of pain. At one stage I started to wonder whether I'd been having myself on all these years—perhaps there wasn't a God. I was agonising, 'God, are you really there?'

This day I managed to drag myself off my bed to do some washing. At the back of where I lived then we had two beautiful gum trees—white trunks, really enormous—and over the years I'd built up a sort of relationship with them. I felt the presence of them whenever I went past, and as I went past this day I looked at one of them and quite spontaneously said, 'Oh, I do love you!' And that was the first time in my life that I'd ever said 'I do love you' to anybody or anything without thinking of getting something back. This was a pure outpouring of love. It really surprised me.

At that instant, as I looked at the tree, it was as if I had X-ray vision—I could see inside the tree—and I could see all these cells working away like mad. As I looked at them I became a cell, and there I was and I had a consciousness. I couldn't think or reason but I had a feeling of joy that I was there doing something to help the universe go round. I was helping bring up all this sap or whatever it was, up into me to pass on to the next one, to the next one to the next one, to the top of the tree. And there was a feeling of joyous participation in something that just went on and on. It was a great feeling but then suddenly I found myself back in my body.

I was so stunned that I started pegging the washing on the line. Then the same thing happened again—I suddenly had this X-ray vision—I could see through all the trees, through everything, and I could see that absolutely everything in the universe was interconnected and interdependent. There was nothing separate, not a thing. Then I saw that even the air between things was just teeming with organisms, and they were all interconnected and all for a purpose. I could see that absolutely everything was interconnected. And I thought, 'So that's how it works!'

I completely lost consciousness of myself—I don't know how long it lasted—then the next thing I knew, I was out in space somewhere, and I knew that the same power that was holding all the planets and everything in space was the same power that was in me. [laughs] You see words don't explain it. I knew there was an absolute reason for being, and I knew that the universe was all one.

When it finished I came back, and it was as if I was numb. Eventually it wore off, but that was the greatest thing that ever happened to me ... My lifestyle today has meaning—it didn't have meaning before. I think I used to feel that I was just drifting along on a current of life, and that I didn't know where I was going or what I was doing. But after that experience I knew there was deep meaning to everything. Everything is connected. Everything has meaning.

In our modern materialistic world it is so easy to move through life without any appreciation for the sacred. Yet as anyone knows who has spent any time alone in a natural environment—even gardening—such proximity to the angels in nature replenishes the soul and opens the heart and eyes to the wonders around us. I remember, one morning, at dawn, in my vegetable garden, feeling a sudden surge of love for a row of snake bean seedlings that were, heads bent over as though in prayer, emerging from the soil into the light of day for the first time. This may seem foolish to some, but when we reconnect to the sacred in the natural world we find spiritual sustenance not only in the beauty of a giant tree and the perfection of a flower, but also in the heroic efforts of the plainest, smallest seed. We cannot help but learn appreciation and gratitude. And, in return, this positive energy can be transmuted into nourishment for the plants around us. Through love and an attitude of piety we are taken into the sacred space of angelic devotions and as we give of ourselves, as we nurture, we are ourselves renewed.

But there is another, even more hidden, aspect to angels since all numinous objects have not only a mundane face but also an esoteric one.

## The esoteric face of angels

The mundane face of angels is already known to all of us since it can be found in the sacred stories of every culture, where their appearance and many roles are clearly described. In recent years we even find their images staring out at us from gift shop windows, greeting cards, movies, and just about every other manifestation of popular culture. But there is also a more mysterious face to angels, available only to the initiated, found in symbols, alchemy and archetypes, in myth and mandalas.

Symbolically, we are told, the angel represents invisible forces ascending and descending between the Divine and the material world. And in alchemy angels are said to symbolise 'sublimation' or, as winged beings, they are said to represent the disembodied.

'Spirit' generally, in alchemy, is almost always related to water, and just as water can be transformed into steam, 'the corporeal' can be transformed into 'the incorporeal'. We see this symbol at work in the trickle of water passed over the head of a baby during the ritual of baptism—a public initiation of the physical child into the world of spirit.

It is important, however, to remember that angels are *more* than just symbols, as powerful as these may be. Through angels it is possible to gain access to transcendental realms and have mystical experiences—the angel in its very numinosity is objectively real as a spiritual phenomenon. But the ineffability of these glorious angel phenomena makes it incredibly difficult to report them in a way that does them justice. However, just as I found when working with near-death experiences, angel experiences are not infinitely variable, but tend to follow certain patterns, and, as Jung suggests, relate to a few basic principles or archetypes.

Jung maintains that even though 'religious images' such as angels may never stand up to rational criticism we should not lose sight of the fact that they are based on 'numinous archetypes'.[29] According to Jung logic can overlook these psychic facts but not eliminate them. Archetypes are primordial thought forms—as ancient as human consciousness itself—and are endlessly repeated throughout time and in every society.

Typical archetypal characters found in mythology and sacred stories throughout the world are the hero, the mother, the goddess, the virgin, the trickster, the shadow. There is the father quest, the saviour who dies, the sacred marriage and the archetype of wholeness, to name but a few. As Joseph Campbell says:

> The images of myth are reflections of the spiritual
> potentialities of every one of us. Through contemplating
> these we evoke their powers in our lives.[30]

One of the most powerful of these primordial images is the circle.[31] The world as circle is experienced every day in the cyclical nature of time, in the inevitable return of the seasons, in the endless cycle of birth, death and rebirth. No beginning, no end.[32] It also represents totality in time and space. Within the circle is a whole world, sealed off from everything outside of it.

A particular kind of circle is a mandala. Typically mandalas (which can be drawn, painted, constructed of coloured sand, danced et cetera) contain what is called a quaternity or multiple of four, often in the form of a cross or square. This 'squaring of the circle' is a common archetypal image and Jung suggests that it could even be called the archetype of wholeness. Indeed it is the basis for all images of God since the central point, circle and quaternity are widely used symbols for the deity. Jung writes:

> In ecclesiastical as in alchemical literature the saying is
> often quoted: 'God is an infinite circle (or sphere)
> whose centre is everywhere and the circumference
> nowhere.'[33]

A mandala may also function as a *yantra*, a simple geometrical design used as an aid to meditation and the development of higher consciousness. Perhaps the best known yantras are the colourful mandalas central to Tibetan Buddhism in which complex details and symbolism are featured.[34]

As a symbol of the self the mandala represents containment of all emotions, impulses and instincts. In psychology, according to Jung, mandalas usually appear in situations of 'psychic confusion and perplexity'. He writes:

> The archetype thereby constellated represents a pattern
> of order which, like a psychological 'view finder'
> marked with a cross or a circle divided into four, is
> superimposed on the psychic chaos so that each content
> falls into place and the weltering confusion is held
> together by the protective circle.[35]

This very much reflects the effect of an angel experience— so often angels first appear at times of spiritual crisis. In the stories that follow, time and again you will see crisis and chaos turn to peace, acceptance, clarity and understanding after an angelic encounter.

It should be clear then, that when we talk about mandalas we are not simply talking of a geometric phenomenon. This particular piece of geometry is *charged* with power and symbolism since always the central point, and the quaternity within the circle represent the ever-present deity.

Rosemary Guiley and Robert Place suggest that the esoteric meaning of the angel is simply that the angel *is* a mandala. They suggest that the angel, as a representative of the divine, is itself a centre of the circle. They also note that in its human-like appearance the body of an angel is symmetrical and can, by outstretching arms and legs, be orientated to four cardinal points which can be joined to form the square and the circle. And, as in Eastern mandalas where every small detail has meaning, the individual details making up angels also have great significance. Their beauty, their wings, the colours that feature in their robes all symbolise far more than would at first be apparent. Once we realise this, the angel becomes a 'charged image' that automatically activates an awareness in consciousness.[36]

When we see angels, not only do we respond to them on a conscious level, but we are seized by the archetype we glimpse, and respond also on an intuitive level. And even if we only read and wonder about angels it still seems that they touch a place deep within us. It seems they connect with the divine light at the very core of our being, opening our inner eyes and hearts.

If you have not yet met an angel, you should not have long to wait.

# 2

# *What Do Angels Really Look Like?*

WE KNOW OF COURSE that angels are not physical beings. We know they are spiritual beings. And although they may at times appear to us *en masse*, they may also separate themselves out as unique individuals with particular features, and even names. So when we ask what they look like, what we are really asking is: How do they manifest to us? In what form do we see them?

Some people *do* actually experience angels as flesh and blood humans —the 'mysterious stranger' is a human form often adopted by angels. For instance, it is said that the Prophet Mohammed was once questioned by a man with very dark hair and a very white face, who he later realised was an angel of Allah. This mysterious man had asked him four questions regarding faith, piety, the pillars of belief for Islam, and the Day of Judgement. After answering these questions correctly, Mohammed was told that, regarding a fifth matter—the timing of the Last Days—the answer was known to no-one but the Creator Himself. Then the man left.[1]

Recently I came across another story which illustrates this mysterious stranger scenario. It appears that one day an eighty-five-year-old woman, Elisabeth, had to do her own shopping, and she was feeling a little nervous about it. However, she managed to get to the supermarket without mishap. She selected her groceries, went through the checkout and was packing up her trolley to go home, when an elderly woman approached and took her by the arm, saying she was there to help her. Elisabeth felt so comfortable with this woman that she even left the trolley with her momentarily while she went off to pay a bill.

As Elisabeth returned to the woman, an incredible sense of peace overwhelmed her and she saw a huge angelic being standing where the woman had been. But as she approached this being, it disappeared and the woman stood in its place. Elisabeth was then led to the carpark where there was a man waiting to drive her home. Without even asking where she lived he drove her right to the door and carried all her groceries inside. Then both strangers disappeared.[2]

This sort of sudden appearance and disappearance is typical of an angelic visitation. Also typical is the calmness and kindness shown to Elisabeth. Angelic visitors always seem to know exactly what is needed, and always seem to appear at exactly the right moment to be of most help.

Some people, however, see angels who, from the outset, are much more obviously spirit-beings, even though they still look somewhat human. Caitlin described an angel she saw during meditation. She said:

He was absolutely stunning. [laughs] I presumed that
angels didn't have a sex but this one was definitely male
and he had really long dark hair and the most gorgeous
face ... He was normal male size and had big six-foot
wings. And I kept thinking to myself, 'Oh, he's
absolutely gorgeous.' I even said it to him, but he just
laughed.

I was surprised when I realised he was a male,
because I'd always thought angels were androgynous or
neither sex. When you see pictures of them they usually
tend to look like women rather than men.

And there was a serenity about him. More than
anything else, that's what I found—peace and serenity.
It was wonderful ... But he was *so* gorgeous!


And Beth, a fifty-six-year-old woman, when describing
the first visit she had from her guardian angel, noted that
although he manifested suddenly in an otherworldly way,
he initially appeared to her as a man dressed in a suit.

He was six foot three tall, and slim, with soft brown
eyes and light brown hair. And he was dressed in a
white suit. *A suit!* Not a startling white—it didn't
dazzle me—but a really nice soft white. And he was
just standing there.

And I said to him, 'If you're a guardian angel, don't
you have wings?' And he just put his arms out to either
side, and said, 'Arms.' And I thought, 'Oh well, okay.'

And then he said, 'When you need me, I am here.
I will stand in front of you, and all you have to do is
walk towards me. I am here for you.'

The next time I was in great distress I remembered this. And straightaway I became aware that he was standing in front of me. So I stepped forward ... I *physically* moved and stepped forward. I remembered that *I* was the one who had to take the first step. And as I took that one step, glorious wings came out from the top of his shoulders. They were made of soft white feathers—like a bird's wing but *very* large.

As I watched, they came out ... and when I took that one step they came in around me. It was the most *incredible* feeling. It was like I was home. You know that feeling? It was unbelievable.

I didn't speak and he didn't say anything. There was no need to say anything. And it was the most beautiful, beautiful feeling. And it went through my mind, 'He *has* got wings!' It seemed to me that the wings *were* there when I was in need. Apparently, the rest of the time he just presents as a normal person with arms. I mean, he's obviously 'light', but he *presents* as a normal person.

Although some people may baulk at the idea of an angel in human form, (especially a human form *wearing a suit*) according to Dionysius, it is quite appropriate to give human descriptions to angels. Indeed he reminds us that the human form can symbolise many of the divine attributes of angels. For instance, the eyes can symbolise the ability to look beyond the earth and behold the light of God; and the shoulders, arms and hands can symbolise the willingness to act in service to the divine will. Similarly, their clothing and the symbols of their purpose such as the lily or the sword can provide a rich source of meaning.[3]

Olivia, who, during a yachting holiday, saw an angel wearing a sou'wester, suggested that his unusual appearance was very fitting under the circumstances.

I had never spent the night on a boat before and I was possibly a little nervous ... Anyway, I woke up in the early hours and I could hear a ship's horn. I just knew I had to get up on deck. I really thought Bob, my son-in-law, would be up there and that something was wrong.

As I came through the hatch I could see a figure at the front of the boat and I really thought it was Bob. I stopped and said, 'Is everything all right, Bob?'

But there was no answer. Then the figure I was looking at got bigger and bigger and bigger until it was about nine feet tall—a man in a yellow sou'wester. There was no face, just darkness, but through him I could see the sails, so I knew he wasn't earthly.

He then told me that we would have a safe journey but three things would go wrong. There would be a bad storm lasting three days and three nights but we'd come through it; the engine would stop during the storm but Bob would get it going again; and we would hit a rock but we'd get back safely and be all right. He then just faded away.

Sure enough it all happened as I'd been told. We hit the storm and it lasted three days and three nights. In the middle of it there was some sort of vacuum block with the diesel and Bob had to suck the diesel through. He was as sick as a dog but he got the motor going so we weren't swamped.

After the storm we came through a reef to a nice
little island and as we were heading to a mooring Bob
said, 'Well, the spook was right about the first two
things but we haven't hit a rock.' At that very moment
we went up on a rock! Bob just gaped at me. We were
towed off and there was no damage done, but
everything I'd been told had happened.

The storm had been pretty severe and we could
easily have gone down but knowing what we did took
the fear out of it. We knew we'd come through okay.

He didn't look much like an angel—he didn't have
soft feathery wings and a golden light—but there was
still a strong feeling of protection. I knew I was
protected and I knew the boat was protected—and that
was a big help at the time. He manifested appropriately
for the occasion. He was there to do a job.

Many years earlier Olivia had also seen a female angel
on two separate occasions. She said:

It was a long time ago, in 1981. It was a pretty
traumatic time in my life and I was in hospital. I
remember coming out of the anaesthetic and I was in a
lot of pain. I looked up and there was a woman's figure
standing in the doorway. I really thought it was one of
the cleaning staff at first—she was wearing a green
gown—but she had really beautiful, golden fluffy hair.
I know how romantic that sounds but that's exactly the
way it was. And she had a very kind, calm face.

She came over to the bed, smiling beautifully at me,
and I was filled with comfort and warmth, and a lot of

other things I needed right then. So I reached out my
hand to her, but the moment I did that she started to
fade. But then even as she faded there was still a lovely
feeling of warmth and healing and comfort left behind.
I knew then that it was an angel. It was very vivid.
I can still see her face.

Then, many years later, my husband was in hospital
having a major operation. I was very concerned about
him because he'd had an adverse reaction to morphine.
After spending all day at the hospital with him, I came
home about half past one in the morning.

After making a cup of coffee I turned around, and
there in the darkened doorway was the same angelic
figure. It was so overwhelming that I just sort of stared.
But I instantly got that same feeling of comfort and
warmth. And at the same moment I got a lot of
information—I *knew* how things were going to work
out. Without words, the information was just there. It
was given from her to me. I blinked and she was gone.

I thought, 'Am I too tired?' I almost disbelieved
what had happened. Then something said, 'Look in the
other doorway.' So I turned and looked, and there she
was again. And she grew and grew and grew till she
was about nine feet tall. It was an incredible experience
it really was. And I thought, 'Well, I can't disbelieve
this!' It was very, very powerful. I felt emotional, but
warm and very peaceful.

All in all it was incredibly thought provoking, and
I didn't get much sleep because I lay awake the whole
night thinking about it. Even though I didn't see any
wings, I knew she was an angel. I could feel her angelic
essence.

Although Olivia was certain that both the man and the woman she saw were angels, some people see angels in a more ethereal form, dressed in diaphanous robes. In 1993 Isabelle, a seventy-eight-year-old woman, was lying on her bed trying to meditate.

It was soon after I'd had shingles. I was doing what I always do, going through a little routine of putting myself in a garden . . . a garden of the spirit. As always I was breathing in the breath of God and breathing out all negativity.

I do this when I go walking too. I breathe out all negativity—resentments or things like that. I breathe them out then I breathe in again. I breathe out any anger or whatever, then breathe in again. But this day I was breathing in the breath of God but I couldn't breathe out any negativity. It really puzzled me. I really couldn't understand it. I kept trying but it just got harder and harder. I couldn't feel it at all— it felt blocked. And I was getting really upset and crying.

Then suddenly, all in one instant, I could see three angels coming down a stairway—I couldn't actually see the stairway—but they were one above the other, and . . . I was almost on a level with them . . . and we were all looking down onto this little creature. I knew it was me but I also knew I was up above, looking down on her. She was sitting on the bed with her knees pulled up, her head resting on her knees, and arms clasped tightly around her legs. I knew I was sitting like that . . . I knew it was me.

The angels were over to her right and I was to her

left. We were all looking down at her. The angels were wearing flowing robes ... I knew they were angels but I couldn't see wings. There was a lot of flowing diaphanous material in a very soft buttercup colour. And I remember it was flowing, sort of softly swirling, anti-clockwise. I remember thinking, 'It's swirling anti-clockwise. I wonder if that means anything.' [laughs]

And Diana, a forty-year-old woman, who was also lying on *her* bed crying, suddenly felt a hand on her arm.

It startled me a bit but I just kept on crying. And then this voice said, 'What's the matter? Why are you crying? What is it? Tell me.'

And I just said, 'I'm sorry. I'm really, really sorry.'

And she said, 'What are you sorry for?'

And I said, 'I'm sorry for my reaction to my mother when I was young.'

She then said, 'Is that all? Anyone in your family would have reacted in the same way.'

At that I opened my eyes to look at her. And standing there was this *huge* being in a brilliant white light. It was the most beautiful thing I've ever seen in my whole life. Words just can't express ...

And I was so shocked ... I *had* actually been having this conversation, and there *was* this pressure on my arm, there *was* someone standing there. And I just looked at her in amazement. But then I sort of pulled back. Even though it was beautiful and uplifting—I knew it was all these things—I still had a moment of fear. She then just sort of went backwards and went away. It seemed as though she thought, 'Oh, I've alarmed her.'

She was *so* tall. Her head was at the ceiling. And her robes ... her robes were like gossamer. I just can't describe them. That's the only word I can come up with. And they were fluid—they weren't just hanging there. It was as though they were in a gentle breeze—there was a sort of movement in them.

She was *so* beautiful, and the light around her was *so* bright. And her robes were a brilliant white but touched by a bluish-purple. Oh, the gossamer of these robes! She was just *beautiful*. And so *tall*.

## Angelic size

Many people comment on the size of the angel they see, and most are astonished at just how tall they can be. A sixteen-year-old boy described an angel he saw during his near-death experience (NDE) as 'about seven feet tall' but although such a size might well seem intimidating, he remarked that he wasn't afraid because he could feel him 'radiating peace and love'.[4] Diana said that the head of the angel she saw reached the ceiling and Olivia described an angel growing before her eyes to about nine feet tall.

But angels sometimes appear as normal adult size and sometimes they can be *much* smaller. Stella, an eighty-year-old woman found herself surrounded by 'tiny, little angels' while she was recovering in hospital from a grave illness. And Caitlin said she has seen angels as small as three inches tall. She said, 'They were *so* tiny!' Jim, a thirty-eight-year-old man, tells of seeing an angel 'dressed in pure white' who was about five feet tall. And Moira, who was concerned about her husband and son flying to Europe at a time when plane hijackings were rife, realised she had nothing to worry about when she saw two angels accompanying them—a tall one with her husband and another smaller one, the same size as her son.

Much taller was the angel seen by Anthea during her near-death experience. She describes what happened:

I was in hospital at the time. It was about a day after I'd had a hysterectomy. I'd picked up an infection and was pretty sick.

I was aware of myself being asleep, then suddenly I found myself going through a tunnel. At the end of the tunnel I met three angels and I knew they were angels because they had wings and were dressed in white and, this may sound ridiculous—one of them was seventy feet tall, and I knew she was because she told me so.

I felt, the whole time I was journeying, that my physical body was not with me, and I was aware of the smallness of my being. I felt very humble. I felt very small, very insignificant, yet I felt very loved at the same time. I was aware of myself as being like a tiny little pinprick, especially when I looked up and saw this towering huge angel in front of me. The other two were about the size of an average human being.

The one who was seventy feet tall was the main angel and she spoke to me. Her voice was very clear and very warm, with a very loving tone. And she said, 'You are with us on the other side. Now you have a choice— you can come with us and we will take you further, or you can go back to where you were. It's up to you.'

I felt really warm and very loved. I felt like I really wanted to be there—it wasn't frightening, just very loving. I really wanted to go with them, because it was so peaceful, so warm and so nice, but I said, 'I'd really love to come, but I can't because I've got work to do.' I also remember saying to them that I had two children and that I wanted to come back to look after my children as well as to work.

And she said to me, 'Okay then, we'll send you back and you'll know that this is not a dream, because when you wake up, the first thing you'll see will be the shape of a cross on your door. You'll know the minute you see the cross that what's happened has been a real experience.' So I remembered that, and when I woke up I saw on the door a very small cross which was made by sunlight through the window. (The window had colonial wooden slats and the cross was made by the sunlight shining through.) The minute I saw it I said, 'Oh, my goodness!' I realised that what'd happened was a real experience. After that, miraculously, the infection turned and I got well.[5]

Rosemary also saw huge angels, who, just as Anthea had said, made her feel incredibly humble and *so* small. She described them as '*enormous* beings of light'.

## Beings of light

Although many people see angels against a background of bright light, some, such as Rosemary, see angels almost

purely *as* light. For instance, Margot, who was giving birth
to her second child at the time of her angel experience,
described what she saw:

> I'd been extremely nervous about this birth because I'd
> had a really hard time with the birth of my first child. I
> really didn't think I could handle the whole thing at all.
> I kept thinking,, 'I'm not going to live through this!'
>
> So during the pregnancy I'd been meditating, and a
> week before the birth I had a breakthrough moment
> where I was no longer afraid and I knew there was a
> presence with me. And I was calm.
>
> It was so easy this birth. I was in this huge bath at
> the Birthing Centre, when I felt this really strong
> presence. It was the presence of overwhelming, all-
> encompassing love. And then I saw them! There were
> four pillars of divine light! [weeps]
>
> I was sort of in a kneeling position and they were to
> my right. There were four of them all standing together.
> I couldn't see arms. I couldn't even make out faces, but
> I knew they were individual presences. There was some
> definition but the light was *so* strong.
>
> I didn't see wings but there was a feeling of face
> and body. Although they were pillars of light I knew
> they had a form—and arms. I absolutely felt arms
> embracing me. It was so overwhelming! And so
> healing! It healed all the traumas of the first birth.
> It was just amazing.

And Valda, an eighty-seven-year-old woman, described
seeing light-beings in a dream just two weeks before the

death of her beloved cat Whanda. She remembers:

> Whanda and I were close companions—she slept on my shoulder every night for sixteen years—so of course when she died I was grief-stricken. But a couple of weeks before Whanda's death I had a wonderful dream.
>
> I dreamed that I took Whanda to what I can only call a heavenly clinic. It was so beautiful and sunny and glowing. And all the staff were angels and so lovely to Whanda and me.
>
> I remember the angels . . . the glow! And there was a beautiful emerald green field, and there were beautiful horses grazing on the grass. And in the centre of the field was a little building, and it was surrounded by unbelievable radiance—a golden, golden glow.
>
> I went into the building with Whanda and the angels. They were all females and they all seemed to be blondes, but there was such a bright golden haze around them that I couldn't distinctly see their features. But they were the essence of compassion and kindness. They offered Whanda a saucer of milk and they said to me, 'You just leave her with us because she's going to be all right now. We're going to look after her.'
>
> That was a wonderful dream. It happened before she died so I was very grateful. That dream was a great comfort to me.

And Beth, a medium, who earlier described her guardian angel as a man in a white suit, said that on one occasion, while working with a client, she saw a strong angelic presence that was quite different. She said:

What I saw with this lady was the most beautiful
golden light. I basically didn't see any features, but I
did see the most glorious golden wings on this being
who was standing behind her. It was a very feminine
energy and the wings went right around her. As I
mentioned this to the lady she cried and cried.

And William Serdahely writes of a woman who, while
meditating, saw a 'vertical column of white-golden light'.
She said that when she merged with the light she felt
'love, peace and ecstasy'.[6] This particular story reminds
me of one of my own early experiences. At the time I
was living in a house overlooking the sea, and one night,
while meditating, I saw a pillar of golden light coming
towards me across the sea. I watched it come from a long
way off, seemingly increasing in size as it approached.
I was amazed as it came straight for me, and as it did I
could see it was made up of millions of tiny little lights.
As it merged into me I felt awestruck. And then, afterwards I found I was left with an incredible sense of peace
and love.

Flower Newhouse taught that angels are easily recognisable to us because they are made up of 'radiant light
energies'. She also wrote that their 'large luminous eyes'
send out the purest form of love.[7] Olivia similarly commented:

The light and the love shows us that it's an angel. And
the *eyes* are so beautiful and soft—they almost seem to

be a dimension on their own—they are quite incredible. And there is so much love there! It's an overwhelmingly loving experience ... but it's also very warmly personal. It's so easy to understand and accept this loving connection with the light.

Indeed people who have had an experience of angelic light-beings often use words such as 'light' and 'love' interchangeably. Raymond Moody writes that these beings of light 'glow with a beautiful and intense luminescence that seems to permeate everything and fill the person with love'.[8] Near-death experiencers in particular often speak in these terms of the light they encounter during an NDE. Olivia, when discussing one of her NDEs said:

I still can't talk about it even now without getting emotional because there was an enormous amount of love there. It was pure love and pure light. That's the only way I can describe it.

And Mary, when describing the three light-beings she saw, said:

They had faces but they didn't have faces—they were luminous. Luminosity, that's the word to describe them. In a way I felt it was the same as love ... it was a lighting up right through everything. It was there, it was here, inside, outside, everywhere. And it was total love, enfolding.

Some years ago I received a letter from Taylor, a twenty-one-year-old woman who had been abused as a child. Taylor wrote:

> I could feel the angels in the room with me whenever
> I needed comfort. It was like being embraced by *light*,
> and so much *love*. I've always thought of it as a natural
> happening, almost like a wonderful reward.

And Fler sent me a description of an angel experience she had, while meditating, at a time of total physical and emotional exhaustion.

> A golden glow began to form in front of my closed
> eyes, and a radiant form became visible within the
> glow ... The angelic being before me was incredibly
> beautiful, decidedly masculine, and his form seemed to
> be made of scintillating golden-white light.
>   At first I thought he had wings, but I soon realised
> they were shimmering, iridescent emanations of light
> shot through with exquisite pulsating colours.
>   His face was like clear, glowing marble, his golden
> eyes were full of love and compassion, and his smile
> was tender as though he knew the stress and exhaustion
> I was suffering.
>   As our gaze met it was as though time stood still and
> I became my true self. A love, warm and wonderful,
> flowed between us. It was a moment of pure and utter
> bliss. A hush descended on my soul and a calm
> receptivity opened up within the very core of my being.
>   Suddenly an incredibly brilliant light, like a star,

shone from his forehead, and swift as an arrow, a shaft
of light shot down, piercing my heart centre with such
an impact that my body jumped, and I cried out.

Then golden energy radiated out and flowed
throughout my whole body. It was as though I was
bathed in the loving energy of God.

All exhaustion left me and I felt I had been renewed.

Fler's experience reminds me of an angelic encounter
described by sixteenth century Spanish nun, St Teresa of
Avila, in her spiritual autobiography.

Beside me on the left hand, appeared an angel in bodily
form, such as I am not in the habit of seeing except
very rarely ... He was not tall, but short, and very
beautiful; and his face was so aflame that he appeared to
be one of the highest rank of angels, who seem to be all
on fire. They must be of the kind called cherubim, but
they do not tell me their names. I know very well that
there is a great difference between some angels and
others, and between these and others still, but I could
not possibly explain it. In his hands I saw a great
golden spear, and at the iron point there appeared to be
a point of fire. This he plunged into my heart several
times so that it penetrated to my entrails. When he
pulled it out, I felt that he took them with it, and left
me utterly consumed with the great love of God.[9]

Many people find it difficult to describe the angel
they see without also describing the emotions that were

an integral part of the total experience. For instance, a woman who was in hospital for an operation was feeling a little apprehensive, when suddenly the words 'I will lift up mine eyes' came to her. As she looked up she was astonished to see something like fine gossamer spreading over her, and with it came a tremendous feeling of total peace.

And Kim and Keith both were aware of an angelic visitor in their bedroom on the night after their three-year-old son, William, passed away. Keith said he could *feel* the presence in the room with them but he couldn't see it. And Kim said:

> She was at the end of our bed and she was throwing
> something over us ... to give us comfort, I think. But
> the presence was there and it was very strong, and I'll
> never forget what she looked like. She was just so
> beautiful ... Just perfection. Just all compassion.[10]

Seeing angels is always an emotional experience, whether they are imposing beings of light, ethereal human-like forms, huge angels, tiny angels, or angels who look just like you or me. Indeed it seems that the very idea of angels—whether we have seen them or not—has captured a place in the human heart. Throughout the ages poets have always used angel imagery, writers of pop songs have continued the tradition in more recent times, and artists seem to have found them an endless source of inspiration.

## Angels in Art

In every society and religious tradition, angels have always had a place in artistic expression. And even if we restrict ourselves, and look only within western art, we see that even here, angels have been depicted in many different forms. On the one hand we see Peter Paul Rubens's friendly little cherubs, and on the other, Albrecht Dürer's fierce, avenging, sword-wielding warriors. Whereas Rubens presents us with a collection of lively, winged baby figures arranged in a devotional 'garland' around the Virgin and child[11], Dürer's woodcuts brilliantly bring to life the apocalyptic visions described in the biblical Book of Revelation.

It is in the Book of Revelation that the mysteries of the world's future are unveiled, and vividly described, in a complex of ideas that seem to be irresistible to the artistic imagination. We read of a bitter, cruel hell for the wicked and a light-filled paradise for the faithful. And this message of retribution and redemption—'fire and brimstone' and 'streets paved with gold'—is mediated at every point by the presence of angels, sharply etched in every detail.

For instance, in Revelation 19 we are told of an 'angel standing in the sun' who, with a loud voice, 'called to all the birds that fly in midheaven'. The English artist J.M. William Turner in the mid-nineteenth century painted an interpretation of this verse in which we see a canvas filled with movement and explosions of golden light. An angelic figure with white-feathered wings stands eyes raised, arms gesturing upwards, calling out to a flock of birds swirling overhead.

There is also an astonishingly beautiful portrayal of this

same angel in a Spanish illuminated manuscript originally compiled in the eighth century by Beatus, a monk at the monastery of Liébana. Many illuminated copies of Beatus's *Commentary on the Apocalypse* were made in the following centuries, more than twenty of which still survive today in collections around the world.[12] Painted in Mozarabic style (a combination of Carolingian, Islamic, Byzantine and Visigothic art) the angel is literally standing in a sun of brilliant red and gold, his arms outstretched, bright blue wings unfurled above his haloed head.[13]

In *The Devil Chained in the Abyss* we see another blue-winged Beatus angel wearing colourful striped robes watching over the devil, who, arms chained behind his back, is seemingly imprisoned in a squared off area of the manuscript page. And in William Blake's early nineteenth-century interpretation of the same biblical verse we are shown a near-naked, muscular angel firmly holding a heavily chained dragon-devil who is about to be cast into the bottomless pit.

We see many portrayals through the ages of the 'seven angels' of Revelations. Depicted colourfully robed, we find them playing their harps in a French illuminated manuscript of the late thirteenth century. In a fourteenth century French tapestry, *The Apocalypse of Angers*, we see the seven angels, seated on clouds, holding their flasks. We see them carved in stone, trumpets to their lips, on the west portal of Notre-Dame Cathedral in Paris. And in a fifteenth-century Flemish manuscript on vellum we see the fifth angel sounding the trumpet. With shoulder-length fair hair held in place by a simple gold circlet this fifth angel is portrayed as an androgynous figure standing in the air, robed in gold, a red-lined cloak floating out just in front of fully-spread white wings.[14]

Other parts of the Bible, though mentioning angels quite often, rarely give the rich descriptions we find in the Book of Revelation. Indeed elsewhere in the Bible we seldom find more than a hint as to what they might have looked like. In some situations, as I've already mentioned, they appeared as men: to Abraham under the oaks of Mamre, to Lot at the gates of Sodom, and as a travelling companion to Tobias.

In Luke 2:9 we are told that an angel of the Lord[15] suddenly appeared before the shepherds to announce the birth of a Saviour. But we learn nothing of this angel's appearance other than that 'the glory of the Lord' shone around them. The angel of the Lord also appeared to Moses 'in a flame of fire out of a bush' (Exodus 3:2). And an angel, drawn sword in hand, appeared before Balaam and his donkey.

In Acts (1:9-10) we are told only that as the disciples watched, Jesus was lifted up into heaven, and two men 'in white robes' suddenly appeared before them. By contrast, in Revelation 18 an 'angel coming down from heaven' is described as 'having great authority; and the earth was made bright with his splendor'. And, even more vividly, in Revelation 10 another 'mighty angel coming down from heaven' is described as 'wrapped in a cloud, with a rainbow over his head; his face was like the sun, and his legs like pillars of fire … Setting his right foot on the sea and his left foot on the land, he gave a great shout, like a lion roaring'.

Two angels named in the Bible—Michael and Gabriel—have, over time, been portrayed so often in art that certain visual conventions have developed to make their presence more obvious to us. Michael, the warrior angel who fights the forces of evil, is perhaps the best known of angels and is usually portrayed winged, wearing armour and holding an unsheathed sword in one hand.

In many paintings Michael, as a symbol of the triumph of good over evil, is depicted standing over the defeated Dragon-Satan with his sword or lance piercing the beast's head. He is also often portrayed carrying a set of scales on which he weighs the souls of those about to die. Christians invoke Michael as the benevolent angel of death, and call on him to deliver and lead them into the eternal light. In Islamic writings he is known as Mika'il and in the earliest traditions of Muslim lore he is said to be 'covered with saffron hairs, each of them containing a million faces and mouths and as many tongues which, in a million dialects, implore the pardon of Allah'.[16]

Gabriel, the angel of the annunciation, figures in countless paintings, particularly during the Renaissance. It is sometimes suggested that Gabriel is the only female archangel, but whether or not this is true, in every tradition he is seen to possess a feminine beauty and is usually depicted as an exceptionally comely, sweet-faced, androgynous youth. Beautifully winged and gowned, he is often seen to be kneeling, holding out a lily (a symbol of purity) as he announces to the Virgin Mary that she will give birth to the child of God.

Gabriel, known in Islamic teachings as Djibril, also appeared to the Prophet Mohammed and, with a face of radiant brightness, dictated the Koran to him, *sura*[17] by *sura*. In his more cosmic manifestations to Mohammed, Gabriel was awe-inspiring—his wings stretched from the east to the west, the sun was between his eyes—but in icons and late medieval paintings he tended to appear in his more usual form. The Sufi, Ruzbehan Baqli described Gabriel as 'the most beautiful of Angels' . . . 'like the moon amongst the stars'.[18]

Over the centuries, the development of certain visual conventions has also made particular classes of angels instantly recognisable to us. For instance, the Cherubim, who had their origins in the *Kerubim*—the powerful guardian figures placed at the entrance of ancient Assyrian palaces and temples[19]—only later became known as heavenly spirits. Even in ancient Israelite lore, heavily influenced by Assyrian images of Kerubim, the cherubim were not considered to be angelic, but rather, fearsome figures who stood guard at the entrance to paradise.

In the Bible the cherubim are the first angels mentioned. In Genesis they are to be found, flaming sword in hand, guarding the Tree of Life in the Garden of Eden. In Ezekial they are seen to have four faces and four wings and in Revelation 4 they are described as 'living creatures' with six wings and 'full of eyes'. It is difficult to imagine how these powerful, sword-wielding figures could have ever been reduced to the child-like creatures we find in nineteenth century art accompanying young women, as symbols of their innocence. However, in Byzantine and medieval art we can already see the cherubim losing their more fearsome features. From that time on, they were depicted by many artists as little more than stylised faces surrounded by four wings. And by the time of the Renaissance they had evolved into the playful little figures known as 'cherubs'.

The Seraphim, by contrast, are almost always depicted as grand six-winged beings, often accompanied by fiery wheels known as the Ophanim or Thrones. Sometimes a Seraph's six wings are simply added to a quasi-human form but other less anthropomorphic depictions show Seraphim as undoubtedly otherworldly creatures. For instance, a sixth-century bronze mirror found in Aleppo shows a face embedded in a solid six-winged form. All six wings issue from the shoulder region—the two upper wings cross above the face, two middle wings extend, one to either side, leaving the hands visible, and the two lower wings fold over in front of the legs so that only the feet can be seen. On either side stand the fiery Ophanim in attendance.[20] Seraphim are portrayed in a similar manner on a vaulted ceiling in the Cathedral of Cefalù, Sicily, but there the feathers of the wings are beautifully differentiated, coloured and covered with many eyes; the full head of each Seraph is clearly defined and each Seraph's right hand holds a sceptre.[21]

St Francis is often called 'seraphic' because he is believed to have been initiated and protected by one of the Seraphim. In a miniature taken from a manuscript compiled circa 1300 by Jacobus de Voragine, we see St Francis kneeling, receiving the stigmata from a Seraph depicted in the usual six-winged form, but with arms raised and feet standing on a fiery wheel, as though propelled there directly from God.[22]

The many works depicting angels through the centuries, however, reflect more than just changing artistic conventions—they also reflect changing ideas about the very nature of these otherworldly creatures, and their role in the divine plan on earth. Nancy Grubb notes that over time angel imagery progressed from the floating, ethereal, translucent figures of medieval art to more earthly, flesh and blood angels solidly situated within a human environment. It is no accident that this change in visual convention corresponded to a parallel movement in western culture from a ready belief in unseen worlds to a more insistent reliance on direct observation and an increasingly strident demand for material evidence. It is ironical however that, over time, the more we in the west distanced ourselves from a belief in angels, the more believably have they been portrayed.[23]

But one thing is clear: whenever and wherever they were depicted, angels usually appeared in the cultural clothing familiar to the visionaries and artists recording their presence. For instance, in an eighteenth century painting by Hanabusa Itcho we see Bugaku dancers with traditional Japanese whitened faces and elaborately decorated black hair, dressed as angels. The train of their patterned silk kimonos is shown flowing behind them under beautifully detailed wings with trailing tail feathers.

In a Persian miniature from Firdowsi's 'Shahnameh' an angel in brightly-coloured Persian garb is shown flying. And illustrated in a sixteenth century Persian manuscript is the famous night journey taken by Mohammed when he was carried to heaven on the back of the Buraq (a mule-like animal with the head of an angel), accompanied by Djibril (Gabriel), and surrounded by a host of attendant angels.[24]

Hindu *apsaras* (angelic figures who accompany slain warriors to heaven) are shown dancing in paradise, forming a circle around the ceiling of an Indian palace. They are winged, crowned, and wearing individually distinct, brilliantly coloured traditional Indian robes.[25] And in my home I have a Balinese angel hanging from the ceiling. She is carved in wood and painted with distinctively Balinese features and dress. She has a fish-like tail instead of feet and looks for all the world like a flying mermaid.

Black Elk, a Holy Man of the Oglala Sioux, painted a picture of two winged angel-spirits who escorted him to the Other World during a near-death experience. These two angels are dressed Native American-style in loincloth and feathered headband, each holding a spear decorated with feathers. Black Elk described them as 'coming from the east, head first like arrows flying, and between them rose the daybreak star'.[26]

In shamanic cultures throughout the world, winged spirits may also take the form of great birds such as Eagle, Raven and Crow, as well as other animals such as Bear, Mountain Lion, Tiger and Horse. As a shamanic practitioner, I have met them in many forms. I shall discuss my shamanic meetings with angels in a later chapter, but for now I would like to tell you of an encounter I had while doing a shamanic journey for a woman I had never met.

During the journey I was greeted by an angel unlike any I had come across before. She was of solid build, had thick, dark brown hair and her face had the features found in Pacific Island cultures. Later, I called the woman and described what I had seen during the shamanic journey. She revealed, with some emotion, that she was of Samoan origin, and that the appearance of a Samoan angel was especially meaningful for her.


In ancient cultures we see the portrayal of many winged creatures and winged humanlike forms. For the ancient Greeks and Romans, Sleep and Death were both portrayed as angels, as were Fate and Victory. Eros, God of Love, found on an Etruscan mirror (c.500BC), was depicted as a beautiful winged youth carrying in his right hand a rose and in his left, a lyre. And in imagery more closely identified with the Roman Cupid, Eros was also often portrayed as a beautiful but mischievous winged boy, who carried a bow and arrow, which he would shoot at gods and men alike. Indeed the Cupids we find in Roman mosaics and frescoes appear to be the forerunners of the little cherubs and *putti* (Italian for 'little boys'), the plump, rosy-bottomed, little figures who later decorate Christian art.

Isis, who was known in Egyptian scriptures as Mother—'the Goddess from whom all becoming arose'—was sometimes addressed as 'thou bearer of wings, thou lady of the red apparel.'[27] And surviving images of Isis powerfully reflect this description as we find her clad in red, kneeling, wings outstretched, ready to enfold her devotee.

And Ahura Mazda, the Wise Lord or God of the ancient religion of Zoroastrianism[28] and his six *amesha spentas* or archangels were all portrayed as powerful, bearded, wide-winged angels. Carved in stone, their monumental features adorned the walls of Assyrian palaces, and in Persepolis the imposing winged image of Ahura Mazda was found carved into one of the palace gateways.[29]

There is no doubt that, whether depicted by artist or sculptor, wings are often a major feature of the angels we find in works of art through the centuries. And, right up to the present day, wings are almost always commented on by people who have had angel experiences. Some comment on their absence but others give descriptions rich in colour and imagery.

## Angel Wings

Sir William Barrett in his classic book, *Death-Bed Visions*, tells the story of Daisy Dryden, a ten-year-old child who died in 1864. Apparently, during her last days Daisy loved to listen to her sister, Lulu, sing for her from the Sunday School song-book. When Lulu had finished singing one particular song which implored the angels to 'bear me away on your snowy wings', Daisy exclaimed:

> Oh, Lulu, is it not strange? We always thought the angels had wings! But it is a mistake; they don't have any.[30]

And Daisy is not alone in this discovery. Kayla, a seven-year-old child I interviewed, was also adamant that angels don't have wings. And June, a fifty-year-old woman, who, throughout her childhood had a 'lovely lady' come and tuck her into bed each night, said:

> As a young child I wondered where her wings were. She never seemed to walk up to me, but rather floated across the room. She didn't wear a long white robe, or have wings, like in pictures of angels, but I can't see why she could not have been one. After all I have heard that not all angels appear like the conventional pictures show them to be. To me she was very beautiful, tall, slim and elegant with the sweetest smile one ever saw. And she seemed to radiate a wonderful silver-white light all around her. All my life the memory of her has been with me.

Swedenborg also saw angels without wings, saying they resembled extremely beautiful human beings. And Kenneth Ring relates the story of a woman, who, after suffering devastating injuries during a motorcycle accident, was fervently praying for God to take her life when she suddenly found herself out of her body in the company of a glorious 'radiant being bathed in a shimmering white glow'. She later noted that although he flew, this magnificent being had no wings.[31]

On the other hand, it is said that as a child William Blake saw a tree filled with angels who 'waved their radiant wings in the branches'.[32] And Juliet, a forty-six-year-old woman, heard the sound of wings flapping at the time of her NDE.

> It was under surgery—a bladder repair operation. I was in the theatre and I could feel myself going to sleep. Then there was a noise, like wings flapping ... and there was this feeling of being pulled very quickly along.

And Olivia related an experience she had one night while leading a meditation group. She said:

> One person in the group had terminal cancer—unfortunately she died two days later. I hadn't been talking about angels but several people in the group that night had the impression of wings, soft wings. It was almost as though you could hear the wings and feel them. I was aware that I could sense the wings around—soft and glowing and filled with light. And they seemed to centre around this woman who was

sitting on the sofa. She had cancer in her breasts and lungs so she was in a bad way. But when she left that night she could walk straight, and she said when she got home she had six hours sleep without pain. So obviously it helped her in some way.

And Genevieve, a nine-year-old child, told me about the angels she saw during a near-death experience.

When I went to heaven I passed all these angels and I drew a picture of them. There was this gate and there was an angel standing on one side of the gate and an angel on the other. Then I went inside the gate and I saw all these angels just floating around the place. Everything was gold and silver.

All the different angels had different kinds of wings. And when they were standing, their wings were huge— they came right down so you couldn't see their feet. And they had light all around them. They had gowns on that looked a little bit like dresses [giggles] and they had light around their heads, sort of like Christians.

Another child, a twelve-year-old girl, who first saw her angel during a near-death experience said the angel she saw had wings of all sorts of colours mixed together, 'all the feathers with a shine, very pretty'. And Moira, a seventy-two-year-old woman, described a series of visions she had which began by focusing on one angel wing:

This beautiful angel came for the first time when I moved here. I'd had a feeling about him being there

before, but it wasn't until I was on my own, where
I could really sit and meditate, that I saw him.

During meditation, the first thing I saw was an
outline of the top of a wing where it comes from the
shoulder. I looked at it, and as I looked, it grew whiter
and stronger and it was lovely, white and feathery, but
with great strength. And it was attached to a shoulder.
That's all I could see at first, but it still left me with a
*wonderful* feeling.

As the months went on, and then the years, I saw
more and more of him. At first I saw the shoulder and
then the side of his face—it was shining wonderfully.
And I saw that he had fair hair, nice fair hair that hung
perfectly straight. He looked like a strong man, there
was nothing effeminate about him. He was very strong
but very shining, with goodness radiating from him.

And then gradually I saw the other wing. And then I
began to see both beautiful wings. I wanted to see all of
him but I had the feeling I was not quite ready. Perhaps
I was still spiritually unfolding on another level.

But now, four years later, I can see most of him.
And when I see him I think of the story of the
transfiguration, where the figures on the mount were
shining and ethereal. I've had a few glimpses of him
full-length, but then he's gone.

He always appeared when I was very sick. I had the
feeling I was being loved and cared for, no matter what.
Whatever I was going through on this plane, he was
there for me.

With this angel I get a feeling of magnificent strength
and it's interesting that I first got that from seeing the
wing—just that bit that goes to the shoulder. There was

tremendous strength in there. And I could feel the
power of it. It was wonderful.

A thirty-eight-year-old man described an angel he saw,
who also had very prominent wings:

There were three angels, the big one and two others.
The big one really stood out, he was so large, over
seven feet tall and the others were normal size like
ourselves. The wings were stone grey colour and you
could see the feathers, which were large. And you could
see where they overlapped.

Some people become very technical in their descriptions
of angel wings. Indeed, one man even reported a conversation he had with an archangel during which it was explained
to him in great detail how wings worked. He said he was
shown how the muscles controlling the wings extended
from the buttocks all the way up the spine. He was also told
that the wings operated quite independently of the arms and
were very long, almost reaching to the ground. And when
the wings were at rest, rather than standing out at the sides
as so often seen in plaster statues, the wings were shaped in
such a way so they sat flat against the body.[33]
For most people, however, the technical specifications of
wings fade into insignificance when compared with the
emotional impact of their angel experience as a whole. And
for those who actually feel the wings fold around them,
the specifics of their construction is the last thing on their
minds. For instance, a sixty-year-old woman, Meg, who
was going through a very difficult time in her life, was

brought to her knees one morning by the realisation that she might even lose her home. She remembered:

> When the realisation of my situation hit me I just burst into tears. Suddenly I felt a gentle presence behind me and two big wings enfolded me. It was as gentle a feeling as could be . . . I then knew that everything would turn out for the best.

And Olivia said:

> At the end of last year I was fairly close to burnout and I was very tired. I went to bed and there was this swirling light around me, and then very soft wings. I can still feel them as I'm sitting here talking . . . The words I got were, 'My wings enfold thee'. And it was as though the wings had folded around me like a blanket. It was an incredible feeling, this lovely soft glowing light and the softness of the wings.

And Kelly, a fifty-one-year-old woman, explains:

> I felt as if I was actually being wrapped in wings. Total love, involvement and enfoldment. A *melting* feeling. Wings that felt like a cloak of blue velvet, that not only wrapped around me but became one with me.

It is sometimes said that angels' wings are not actually 'wings' but are their vividly-coloured auras—the constantly moving light energy that surrounds their bodies. It is also often remarked that angels don't need wings to move about anyway as they are able to move anywhere they want simply by willing it. This may well be so but there is no doubt that wings have been a persistent feature of angel imagery throughout the ages. And certainly for those who have had a direct experience of angel wings nothing could convince them that they do not exist. If angels are in their essence light-beings why should they not manifest with wings? After all, the imagery of wings is rich in symbolism and even for those who have not had a direct experience of angels, wings may still represent many spiritual qualities and abilities. Wings may symbolise the ability to fly and move between physical and non-physical realms. They may even represent effortlessness and trust and divine purpose. For those of us firmly earthbound, the image of wings and the golden light that accompanies them can be very inspiring. It can literally fill us with spirit.

So, what do angels *really* look like? And how do we know they are angels? When I asked Rene, a twelve-year-old girl who has seen many angels since her NDE, she just chuckled and said:

> I know they are angels when I see them because they
> have their robes on and wear the wings. And anyway
> they look different from normal people because they
> have paler faces and beautiful eyes ... and sometimes
> they even change into different forms like light ... And
> when I see them they are very peaceful and loving, and
> I feel really nice and warm.

Angels. Wings, beauty, light, love, peace and warmth: that just about sums it up.

# 3

# *How Do We Meet Angels?*

ONE THING I HAVE learned over the years is that there is nothing in particular we need to do to bring angels into our lives since they are always there for us, whether we are aware of it or not. However, if we are open and still enough to receive their communications we can meet with them by various means. The first is by taking notice of our dreams.

## *Dreams*

Six or seven years ago just before Christmas I had an unusual dream. During this dream I moved into a new home that was very old and solidly built of stone, very beautiful and, best of all, situated on a clifftop overlooking the sea. A voice told me that the name of this home was to be 'Ramparts', a rather surprising choice. Although somewhat puzzled by this name I accepted what I was told. I made a tour of my new home, enjoying every beautiful detail of it. And then the dream faded.

The next morning I recorded the dream in my journal,

puzzled again over the strange name but then got on with my day. Later that morning I was out shopping for Christmas cards. I especially wanted to find cards featuring angels but was having no luck at all. I searched high and low all over the city and still could not find any cards with angels on them. Eventually, on my way home, I stopped off at a little corner store to buy something else and while desultorily flicking through the few cards that were there came across six copies of an exceptionally beautiful card featuring three haloed angels bathed in a golden glow. I thought it was probably a detail taken from a larger painting, done in nineteenth century style, but as I didn't have my reading glasses with me I was unable to read the name of the artist. I bought all six cards.

When I arrived home I immediately reached for my glasses so that I could have a better look at the painting. I turned over the card to read the artist's name—John Melhuish Strudwick (1849–1937). And below the artist's name was the title of the work—The *Ramparts* of God's House! 'Of course!' I thought to myself, '*Angels* are the Ramparts.'

A few months later I had another angel dream. This time I dreamed I was out walking with one of my sons. We had stopped for a while on a low wooden footbridge, which traversed a pond, and were looking into the water below. As we stood there I noticed a large piece of driftwood in the shape of an angel slowly floating to the surface. As I went to lift it out of the water, my son asked why I wanted it and I answered, 'I want to have angel wings on my house.'

Dreams are a wonderful way for spiritual messages to get through to us and sometimes I even receive angelic instructions in my dreams. Soon after completing my last book, *Beloved Visitors*, I began receiving many hints and nudges that told me my next book was to be about angels. And one night during a dream I received a definite instruction to 'diarise' my life during the process of research and writing. I was too weary at the time to really understand why, but, feeling rather overwhelmed with emotion—'Why are they talking to *me*?'—I decided to do as I was told. And thank goodness I did because over the following months and years the number of angelic events in my life increased so dramatically that I would never have remembered them without my diary notes.

And the feelings that come with dreams, the emotion and sense of wonder, that overflow into our waking lives, can be just as important as the message they swirl along with them. In point of fact I believe that often the sense of wonderment left in the wake of a dream may actually *be* the message. A similar process can happen in other circumstances too. For instance, I remember, after my near-death experience, having no understanding at all of what had happened to me. Yet I was left with a very strong sense that, whatever it was, it was profoundly significant. Although I had no idea what the significance was, this did nothing to undermine the importance of this event in my life. In my *soul* I knew this was a momentous experience and no amount of discussion, excavation or dissection could change that. My outlook on life was changed forever at a fundamental level.

Similarly, after having the angel dreams, the elation I felt at having this angelic presence in my life stayed with me. Indeed, even when I think back on those dreams today, I still feel a sense of wonder. It is so important not to lose the magic of our dreams by trying to explain them away, or pin them down, or break their code. Rigorous interpretation is not what is needed. Dissecting any of these dreams into their component parts would not be difficult to do, and I'm sure most people would have no difficulty in interpreting the main elements, but how much more rewarding would this be?

As Thomas Moore writes, 'Dreams are the purest form of enchantment'[1] and the value of enchantment is that it takes us away from our habitual ways of seeing the world. It allows us to return to our daily lives richer and fuller— seeing everyday things and events afresh. Becoming aware that there is mystery at the heart of our inner lives is only a source of puzzlement if we feel we have to decipher it. Sometimes, as Thomas Moore suggests, it is better to be enchanted rather than puzzled by the fruits of the soul. Rather than feeling we have to shine a light into their dark corners, we could treat dreams as a form of initiation which *expands* our view of the world.

Robert Kirven, a Swedenborg scholar, relates a dream he had towards the end of World War II. Despite the fact that the Allied victory was close at hand he was still very depressed, and worried about the possibility of an Allied defeat. In *Angels in Action* he writes that in the dream he was standing alone in an open field surrounded, as far as the eye could see, by a massive tangle of barbed wire. Suddenly an angel, appearing as a bright light, came over the hill in front of him, passed straight through the barbed wire, vaporising it as she went, moved past him and out of sight in the other direction. Realising he was now free, he walked off in the direction from which the angel had come. He then woke up to find that his depression and fears about the war had been lifted. Kirven remarks that even without a word being spoken the angelic message had been clear, and his 'experiential certainty' that angels were capable of such things had the added bonus of freeing him from his other fears as well.[2]

## Meditation

It is often said that it is through prayer we talk to God and through meditation that we listen. Thus meditation is an open invitation for angels to communicate with us. And even if they do nothing more than simply allow their presence to be felt, the message that they are there is usually enough to leave us in a blissful state of peace and wellbeing. Beth described one experience she had during meditation:

> At first it was an experience almost of nothingness. And then I seemed to be in the midst of this most incredible light. There was nothing but the light, it was everywhere, all-pervasive. There was nothing to say. It felt just amazing.

And Isabelle said:

> During meditation one afternoon I saw the face of an angel. It was among, but in front of, other faces. It was a rounded, almost plump face, very serene and bathed in gold. It was sort of in a rectangular frame of golden light that separated this one face from the others. I may

have imagined it but I think she was Valeoel or Peace.
She left me feeling so calm and peaceful.

On other occasions angels may give us a glimpse of their
usually unseen activity. For instance, a few years ago I was
quite concerned about a very dear friend, Morgaine, who
was completely burned out through overwork. One day,
while meditating, I was shown an image of her surrounded
by a flurry of white-robed, winged angels, with two of
them, one either side, literally holding her up. As soon as
I'd finished meditating I phoned to let her know what I'd
seen. Then, ten days later I saw Morgaine's angels again.
This time they were all, including the two main angels,
standing back watching her, like concerned parents watching
a toddler take its first steps, ready to swoop in to the rescue
if needed, but allowing her the freedom of finding her own
way.

Angels, however, do not always appear in such a traditional
form. One day I was meditating with three other women
when, unexpectedly, I was shown the angels of each of
them. The first was a huge angel in the form of a luminous
tree with roots going deep into the ground, a long slender
body reaching to a beautiful head hundreds of metres in
the air. The second was a magnificent angel in female form,
about nine feet tall with arms outstretched and palms raised,
face turned upwards, with light pouring out of her in every
direction. I was told that this angel was the Bringer of
Light. And, most surprisingly, when I came to the angel
of my third friend, I was shown three human-sized skimpily-
dressed female angels shoulder to shoulder gleefully dancing
the can-can! After the meditation, I described to each of

the women what I had seen: the huge angel of nature, the magnificent Bringer of Light and ... I felt concerned that the third woman would be disappointed at the frivolous vision I had received for her but when I told her what I'd seen she roared with laughter and was delighted. However odd it may sound to others, we *always* receive exactly what we need.

Dylan, the retired scientist mentioned in Chapter One, who realised he was an alcoholic after an angelic intervention, had an extraordinary experience of purification one day while meditating.

I used to lie down rather than going into the lotus position to meditate. Anyhow I was lying on the bed and I looked up. The room was not very bright but there was this being up in the top left-hand corner of the room looking down at me in a very calm way. I could more or less see the whole body and what it reminded me of was the Magician from the Tarot pack. I didn't know much about Tarot in those days but I had seen one or two packs. He had a very benevolent countenance and was wearing rather showy robes. He was very calm and obviously very powerful. And he was looking down at me.

Suddenly I felt this tingling start at my feet and gradually move quite slowly up my body. The only thing I've ever come across anything like it is what's called 'zone refining' in metallurgy, where you get a bar of fairly pure metal that you want to make very pure, and you pass a radio frequency coil that melts the metal just underneath it. As you gradually pass up the bar, the molten zone sweeps the impurities along with it.

And when you get to the end you stop, turn the radio frequency current off, let it cool down and then chop off the end the impurities are in and you've got a beautiful pure bar of metal.

It seemed to me that something like that was happening to me. This tingling was going all the way up to my head. It got to my head from my feet and just went out and then it started again, and then again. So it happened three times. And then this angelic being just sort of faded away and that was that.

I wasn't frightened in any way. I was surprised that it was happening to me but I just thought, 'Oh well, he knows what he's doing.' I knew absolutely that he was supervising something with regard to me.

By then I'd been three months sober so I'd come to believe in spiritual things for sure. In fact I didn't have to believe, I'd had it demonstrated to me. And this was another demonstration. As I say, I'm one of the few people I know who's got into AA and had a trouble-free run. And I'm sure it's partly due to this sort of thing happening to me. It made me very whole-hearted. It made me realise that the spiritual world is much more powerful than the material world.

I'm sure it happened for a purpose—to purify me. And afterwards I felt very light-hearted.

On some occasions, angels may communicate during meditation to give specific advice. One day, while meditating, I saw angel wings and faces—sweet, young and golden— and I was given a message. At the time I was suffering a painful 'frozen' shoulder, but since I knew from past experience that any form of physical debilitation was a sign for me to be still, I was spending several hours a day in meditation. This particular day I was told I should, as I breathed in, breathe light into the shoulder and as I breathed out, breathe out any anger accumulated there. This would speed up the healing process. I did this on a regular basis for a long time afterwards and always found it helpful.

I often saw angel faces in meditation after that but their messages were not always about healing. Sometimes they just seemed to be there to let me feel their presence but on two separate occasions I was surprised to be told to read a particular book. The first book was *Commune with the Angels* by Jane Howard and that time I was told, 'There is a message in there for you and much to learn and accustom yourself to.'

The second time, about two years later, I was told to read *To Hear the Angels Sing* by Dorothy Maclean. At that stage I was doing a lot of gardening. I had recently moved to a beautiful house in a rainforest area surrounded by five acres of overgrown garden, and I felt compelled to spend as much time as possible at work in it. This was not an onerous task for me but had soon become a source of great joy. It was hard physical labour but it felt like sacred work, as if by tending this huge garden I was honouring the spirit of this land and finding my place within it.

I felt spiritually refreshed and nourished by my hard work and I would often say to friends that I felt I was in heaven, that I had found my true home at last. But as my Higher Self was connecting with my new home, my practical thinking self was constantly nagging me to stop gardening and get to work on my book. I felt torn because both seemed important.

The morning I was told to read Dorothy Maclean's book I was not even aware that it was on my bookshelves—I had bought it a couple of years earlier and had never got around to reading it. But I began reading it that day while sitting outside in the winter sunshine. I was astonished to find that it was all about gardens and the *devas* who enlighten and give life to them. It immediately confirmed for me that this intense period of work in the garden was not just an indulgence. It *was* sacred work and was further developing my connection with angels.

Allowing the book to fall open at whatever I was meant to see, I read that *devas* believe the barriers between our two worlds are breaking down. In messages to Dorothy Maclean they said:

> The initiative for this communion has to come from humans; we are always here. Those of you who do reach to us feel the touch of beauty, of truth, of wonder, and even a sense of homecoming. From this you will know that you have entered our reality and you will wish to come again. You will experience an expansion of spirit, and you will be refreshed.[3]

And, further corroborating my own feelings as I worked in the garden, Maclean noted that the most outstanding characteristic of the devic world was joy. They told her:

> Joy is what we work with, joy is what we are, what you are. Let us show you this, let us show the whole of humanity . . . Throw all conditioning overboard and experience from within. Let the joy roll out and unite you with all life.[4]

After reading this I ran into the house to look in my 'angel diary'. Two years earlier during meditation I had been told to pick up a pen and write down the following message:

You are being forced to take time out for yourself.
Enjoy this. Enjoy your quiet time. Let anxiety go.
Enjoy. 'Enjoy' means to enfold yourself in joy.
Let joy be your nature. Joy *is* your nature. Live it.'

Back outside, I picked up the book again and read:

According to the angels, the natural state of life, including humanity's, is one of overflowing joy. With that joy, we can lift all life.[5]

And, I thought, redress the balance which at times seems to weigh so heavily in favour of suffering and sorrow.

## *Writing*

A third way of receiving angelic communications is through writing. One of the people I interviewed in my research for this book was Lisa, a twenty-nine year-old woman, who receives messages from Angel Raphael which she records through automatic writing. She describes the process:

I generally do a meditation first for relaxation, then at some point during the meditation I hear his voice. He usually says something like, 'Again I am here, and joyous,' or 'Joyous am I to be here again.' Something along those lines. And I get so excited.

I get like a little bubble down in my stomach— 'He's here!' And as I reach for the pen and book to write, that little bubble of joy and love is right there. And then it starts to spread out . . . like a gold-white shimmering love and warmth. And then I feel him at my shoulder. It's as if I'm sitting and writing with somebody standing at my shoulder dictating. I actually feel him there.

And sometimes we take a break . . . it's not like he goes away, but he sort of takes a half step back so that I can gather myself together. It's very tiring doing all that writing and trying to keep up, and trying to comprehend what he's saying, and trying to put it all down. He speaks so fast! Sometimes I tell him, 'Slow down!'

At some point he gives me the message I need to hear right there and then. And then there's a bit of peace and quiet, and we are just quietly together. And I feel such warmth.

The message always ends with 'Joy, love, light and laughter'. Love and light are the same to Raphael: the love of light, the light of love. And joy is another part of light. And laughter is one of the biggest parts. You know how you feel when you laugh—you just feel joyous and you feel wonderful and you feel light and loved. So one of his real big things is laughter.

And when it comes to the end it's sort of like a very soft parting. It's just very gradual. It's like, 'Oh, you've gone.' And it's nice and peaceful.

Sometimes there's a theme—it depends how I am at

the time. Recently I was feeling really down, really, really down, and the whole message was to heal myself, to trust, to love. He was saying he was sad I could no longer see joy and laughter in my life. I was at rock bottom. I was extremely ill, I was in a really horrible job and I'd hit rock bottom—emotionally, physically, the lot. So the messages I got that day were specially for me. But sometimes they are more general . . .

The one thing that peeves him is when I change his words when I'm writing. If I think, 'That's not right, it shouldn't be said that way,' my ear blocks up. It's like someone's stuffed cotton wool in my ear. But then if I think, 'All right, I'll write it your way,' it flows again.

[You physically hear it in your ear?]

Yes. It's always my left ear because that's where he stands. But then again, it's not a voice from outside. It's a voice from in here, from in my heart . . . but it's in my ear as well. It's amazing. I still sometimes have doubt. I still do. But then I think, 'Just accept, just keep going.'

Miranda, a thirty-year-old woman, also receives messages through automatic writing.

About two years ago I had an inkling to try automatic writing and I did it a few times but for the last four months whenever I think I might sit down and do some writing, I start to hear the messages.

And it's wonderful. Whenever I start to write, if I've got any fear or anything like that, it is just diminished and I'm filled with love and calmness. So I know whatever's coming through is very pure ... They always give me such a lot of joy.

I have a special angel, Grace, who often comes through to me. I feel she's the very feminine one who says 'My dear' a lot ... I enjoy that. A lot of the messages are from her but there are also two others and one of these is a very strong protector. I'm sure I've had messages from him before, but he comes through very strongly in the writing. I feel he tries not to be too forceful but he is one of those angels who like to make their point ...

And they're all very strong in telling me to let everybody know that they'll come in whenever they're invited. We need only ask.

I read in a book a while ago that when Pontius Pilate said to Jesus, 'If you're the Son of God, where's your God now?' Jesus answered, 'All I would need to do is pray and a thousand legions of angels would be here.'

I'm not religious but I tell people that all the time. I feel really strongly that one of my main purposes is to tell people that all they need to do is ask and listen, because the angels are always there.

## A sensed presence

Some people meet an angel whose presence, although invisible is tangible nonetheless. For instance, Lisa described sensing the presence of Raphael.

I've never seen Raphael but I can always feel him. I feel his presence. He's over my left shoulder and if I extend my arm up he's taller than that. He's always there,

about four inches away from my shoulder. I always
know he's there, I never see him but I can always feel
his presence. At times I feel him envelop me in his
wings, in love and warmth. I have even seen a gold
light come around me but I've never physically seen
what Raphael looks like. He's just there.

And Kelly described sensing an angelic presence at a time
of distress. She said:

Some years ago, after many years of ups and downs, I
went through a marriage breakup. As you would expect
after such a bereavement, the following week was one
of the lowest ebbs in my life.

One day I was walking by the water alone. By that
stage, I'd realised my income would be reduced by
about seventy-five percent and I was finding that fact a
little difficult to take in on top of the rest. The distress
was a feeling of great loneliness. I felt I was devoid of
every*body* and every*thing*.

At one point I sat down . . . and it was as if I could
feel somebody sit down right beside me. It felt almost
like a breath of air passing very softly down one side.
And at that moment I felt that all I really needed was
exactly what I had right then and there . . .

I've felt people with me before—the very gentle
touches—but never to this extent. I could feel the
presence of a whole body in that very, very, light
feather touch. It wasn't just the touch of a hand, it was
more like the sweep of a whole body.

And it was very calming—enlightening and calming

at the same time. It filled me with a feeling of great positivity. The negative parts seemed to drain away and were replaced with a beautiful feeling of knowing, and acceptance.

Even now, many years later, as I speak of it, the feeling that came with that experience still has the same calming and soothing effect.

## *Waking visions*

Sometimes, we can even meet angels in waking visions. Rosemary, related an extraordinary set of events which culminated in a meeting with Archangel Michael.

In 1993 a friend channelled a rather surprising message for me. I was to go and meet the Archangel Michael in a rainforest on the twentieth of May. Since I'd had the feeling for months that I had to go to Hawaii, it immediately came into my consciousness that the place I had to meet him was a rainforest in Hana Maui.

It was already the tenth of May and not being very affluent I didn't know how I was going to do it ... But things miraculously fell into place and by the eighteenth of May I found myself in Hawaii, which still left me with one day to get over to Hana Maui and prepare myself for the twentieth.

The morning of the nineteenth I was preparing to go to Hana, when a most incredible thing happened—I had the feeling I was going to meet my bridegroom. Then, when the porter arrived to collect my bags—it was the same porter who'd helped me with my luggage when

I arrived—he presented me with the most beautiful lei made of wonderful, fragrant cream flowers. He said he'd felt guided to prepare it specially for me. He'd picked the flowers from his own garden and had spent hours the night before making it. I just burst into tears as he put it around my neck. I felt this was my wedding bouquet.

After a short plane trip I arrived in Hana where I booked into the Sheraton—I didn't know where else to stay. It's situated on sixty-six acres of undulating lawns and they've got these wonderful cottages dotted around. As I opened the door to my cottage—they'd put me in a honeymoon suite—Michael spoke to me and I just fell apart and cried.

On the morning of the twentieth I woke up. I didn't know what was going to happen. At the time there was a lot of talk about Ascension and I didn't know whether I was going to ascend, whether a spaceship was going to take me away [laughs] or what was going to happen, so I left notes for my children.

I took a little disposable camera, a notepad and pencil and I went looking for Michael. I thought, 'I'm not going to find him on the lawns of the Sheraton.' So I walked and walked and walked. Then all of a sudden I felt my hair starting to stand on end, and I looked to my right, and there was this little church—the Church of Salvation! [laughs] Incredible! I went in. I saw fairies and other beings. It was quite overgrown with weeds. I sat in the backyard thinking, 'Am I trespassing? Will somebody come and say to get out of here?'

It had been raining so I sat on a dry banana leaf . . . and nothing happened. After a beautiful meditation of an hour, I thought, 'Have I spent thousands of dollars to come here just to meditate?' [laughs]

So I picked myself up, dusted myself down and went walking again. And as I was walking, the rainforest terrain became a bit thicker—it was near a rather black pebbly beach—and I saw a little track. As I started to walk down this path I saw little angelic beings flying just ahead of me, they were just everywhere. And they said, 'Look, she sees us.' And with that, I suddenly saw Michael. I did not see a sword, I did not see wings, I just saw him—first his head and shoulders, then the rest of him.

I just stood there and I didn't get any closer for ages. I couldn't because I was crying too much. And by this stage the energy was so intense I could hardly breathe. [very emotional]

He said, 'Come and walk with me a while.' [very emotional] And the love! To be loved like that! [weeps] And I walked up to him. And he said, 'Through you many things will come to pass.'

Then something very funny happened. I walked straight into the biggest spider's web you've ever seen [laughs] . . . I was laughing and crying . . . I had spider's web all over me. And I really don't remember a lot after that. I was just in a different state, that's all I can say.

After I left, I remember, I went into a building. I needed tissues so I got some toilet paper to wipe my face and eyes. And I cried for three days after that, just from the overwhelming love. And from that point on, I don't think my life was ever the same.

## *Angel-led excursions between worlds*

Occasionally we can open ourselves sufficiently to angelic energy for an angel to take us on a short excursion or voyage of discovery. Although these excursions are enjoyable in themselves, there is almost always a lesson to be learned from them—if only that angels are constantly there for us. Jim described a time when, during meditation, an angel took him out through the ceiling.

She was in pure white, everything about her was white, and she was possibly five feet tall and she had her hand out like this and she just took me up.

I thought I wasn't going to be able to get out the ceiling but she just took me along the ceiling and then *pop* straight through! Straight out! [laughs] Oh heck, I'm still trying ... Because I'm a very analytical person it's very hard for me to break through my thought barriers. After all, everything physical has got rules about it and you can't just go through things like that!

Anyway, she took me out to show me a larger picture of what this earth is about. She took me out to see the globe and to show me that I shouldn't get stuck in the physical. We didn't stay out long—she probably thought I'd seen enough and got the message that I was not to confine myself within these kind of walls. And I'm sure she also tried to reinforce for me that the earth is such a pretty place.

It was an amazing experience being with her. I felt so close to her, it was almost as if we were one.

As we have already seen, many angels come into our world but there are also occasions, for instance during near-death experiences or shamanic journeys, when the meeting is an otherworldly one and takes place in the world of angels.

## *The shamanic journey*

Shamanism is a mystical practice and a healing tradition that has existed for tens of thousands of years in tribal cultures throughout the world. Western missionaries and colonial administrators tended to dismiss shamans as witch-doctors and sorcerers but they are, in fact, seers, healers, doctors of the soul, guides and counsellors held in high esteem by the society within which they work.

Although such healers were almost completely eliminated in Europe during the Middle Ages, shamans have continuously practised up to the present day in many other cultures, from Siberia, to North America, to Africa, to Asia and Australia.

Puzzling to some is the widespread resurgence of shamanism throughout the world today even in the west. Michael Harner, anthropologist, shaman and teacher of shamanism, suggests that there are many factors contributing to this revival, such as the development of wholistic health practices for healing and wellness and the reverence shamanism embodies for the earth and all its inhabitants.[6]

As I travel around the country I see a thirst for a truly spiritual focus in life and a desire for direct, first-hand experiences. I often, for example, have people tell me, after reading or hearing about the impact NDEs have on people's lives, that they wish they could have a near-death experience themselves. There's no doubt those who have had an NDE are completely changed by it. But I have similarly seen people deeply moved by the profound nature of their first shamanic journey—so I would add that possibly the most compelling reason for the resurgence of shamanism is that, as a direct experience of the spiritual realm, it really works.

However, shamanism is not a game and neither is it a party trick or form of fortune telling. I always emphasise that shamanism is *sacred* work and not to be undertaken lightly.

Michael Harner writes:

> A shaman is a man or woman who enters an altered
> state of consciousness—at will—to contact and utilize
> an ordinarily hidden reality in order to acquire
> knowledge, power, and to help other people.[7]

This altered state has been called by Harner the 'shamanic state of consciousness' and is most often reached by the use of a monotonous, prolonged, percussive beat—usually drumming.[8]

This shamanic state of consciousness is made up not only of a transcendent state of awareness but also of knowledge. For instance, once in a shamanic state of consciousness it is important to know how to gain access to the non-ordinary world and what to expect in terms of geography and inhabitants once it is reached. For example, if a shaman is entering non-ordinary reality to retrieve a person's lost power (in the form of his or her 'power animal'), it is important for the shaman to know where to go, how to identify the right 'animal' and how to return it to the client.

That is, it is important to be familiar with shamanic methods and cosmology.

According to the shamanic world view, non-ordinary reality is made up of three distinct territories: the Lowerworld, the Middleworld, and the Upperworld. This is not a hierarchy. These names simply indicate the direction the shaman must travel in order to reach them.

The Lowerworld is the world of nature. There the shaman will see and travel through a wide variety of landscapes—anything from deserts to tropical jungles, high mountains to rivers to beaches. For instance, at times I will begin a journey from a position high in the mountains then find myself flying over valleys, deserts and even the sea (depending on the purpose of the journey). It is also in the Lowerworld that the shaman will meet and call on the assistance of 'power animals', helping spirits which can be in the form of animals, birds, reptiles or occasionally even insects.

The Middleworld is physically very much like the world around us, except that the shaman is seeing it while in an altered state. It is also outside of time. It is towards the Middleworld that I often feel drawn when doing soul retrievals since it is there that I will see the scene that precipitated the departure of the lost soul part. But then I may need to go somewhere entirely different in order to retrieve it.

The Upperworld is the world of angels, teachers and other enlightened beings. It is a very ethereal world. It sounds like a cliché but I see it as a world of white or pastel clouds, of light, of colours, of joy and peace. Here I have seen dozens of angels behaving in all sorts of ways—from rollicking, fun-loving child angels to calm, reverent angels standing in small groups ready to give me advice. I have had conversations with individual angels and have quite often, over the past few years, been given guidance by one particular enlightened being.

There are no shamanic rules to define what these worlds look like so each shaman learns from his or her own personal experience.

Although shamanic practices have evolved in cultures completely isolated from each other the methodology that has developed is incredibly similar. A feature that distinguishes shamanism from any other form of healing and guidance, as you may already have guessed, is the use of the shamanic journey.

To embark on a shamanic journey the shaman will first enter the shamanic state of consciousness, as I've already mentioned, with the aid of, for example, drumming. He or she will then leave their body and journey into nonordinary reality in order to accomplish a particular mission.

Several people have pointed to the similarity between near-death experiences and the shamanic journey—the leaving of the body, travel through a transitional realm (such as a dark tunnel) towards a light, and entry into another world. Although I agree with this in principle, there are many differences—a very obvious one being that it is possible to engage in a shamanic journey at any time, whereas it is necessary to be at least momentarily close to death to have a near-death experience.

One connection, however, is acknowledged in traditional cultures, where a near-death experience can sometimes be a direct initiation into shamanism. There are many examples in the literature of shamans who became aware of their vocation as a result of a near-death experience. Black Elk, a Holy Man of the Oglala Sioux, is a prime example.

During a serious illness at the age of nine, Black Elk saw two winged beings coming from the clouds to fetch him, saying, 'Hurry! Come! Your Grandfathers are calling you!'

Leaving his body behind in the care of his parents, he followed these beings into the other world, where he was shown and taught many things. He said: 'And while I stood there I saw more than I can tell and I understood more than I saw; for I was seeing in a sacred manner.'

At one point he was given the 'herb of understanding' and he was told: 'With this on earth you shall undertake anything and do it.' He was then told to drop this sacred herb onto the earth and, as he watched, it took root, grew and flowered.

As the time approached for his journey to come to an end, the oldest of the Grandfathers told him, 'Now you shall go back with power to the place from whence you came ...' And as he returned to his body Black Elk could see 'the face of the day ... with the daybreak star upon its forehead.' He saw the sun leap up and look upon him and he could hear the sun singing a sacred song. By the time the singing ended he found himself looking down on his parents tending a sick boy. He said, 'Then I was sitting up; and I was sad because my mother and father didn't seem to know I had been so far away.'9

Of course there can be other methods of initiation but they almost always include a death-rebirth experience— whether literal or metaphorical—and there are always significant visions.

I am not saying that all near-death experiencers are

shamans—far from it. But it is true to say that a near-death experience provides a spiritual opening which can lead one to choose a healing path. In my research over more than ten years I have found that many near-death experiencers, having no fear of death, retrain as workers in the healing professions, or work with the dying and grieving as volunteers in hospices. However, for me, the healing path has been a shamanic one.

It is extremely important when doing a shamanic journey to have a very clear intention, to be crystal clear about the purpose of the journey. When using the journey for guidance or counselling, I often say to my clients that the clearer they can be about the questions they want to ask, the clearer the answers will be. However, sometimes people are so confused, depressed and immobilised in their lives that they are unable to formulate questions. In that case I simply ask their helping spirits in non-ordinary reality—both angels and power animals—for words of guidance that can be of some help to them at that particular time.[10]

It is difficult to describe a typical shamanic journey since they are never the same. Even in terms of gaining access to the different worlds, different approaches are taken. However, that said, the most straightforward and easiest form of shamanic journey to learn is the journey to the Lowerworld.

Once in the shamanic state of consciousness, to get to the Lowerworld the shaman enters the earth. The entrance could be the hole of a burrowing animal, a hollow tree, a cave or even a pond. The important thing is that, once inside the entrance to the earth, the shaman travels downwards until she or he emerges into the light of the other world. It is there that the shaman comes out into a landscape and meets his or her 'power animal' before setting off to fulfil the purpose of the journey.

It is difficult to be much more specific than this. Although journeys usually follow a similar pattern up to that point, once in the other world anything can happen. And does. But one thing I have learned, is to trust that whatever is needed at any particular time will unfold.

By contrast, to go to the Upperworld it is necessary to rise. Sometimes I find myself wafting upwards on a spiral of smoke, moving up a rainbow or being drawn upwards by angels. The first time I went to the Upperworld it took me by surprise. I had begun my journey in the usual way, expecting to go to the Lowerworld but suddenly there was a rainbow in front of me and I found I was sliding upwards along it. Quite quickly I reached the top of some clouds and there I found a ladder. As I continued upwards I began to have the sense that there were two angels accompanying me. When I came out at the top there was a whole flurry of little angels who flew around excitedly.

These child-like little angels and the two taller angels wanted to take me somewhere so I let myself be led, enjoying the feeling of being drawn along in a slipstream of sparkling light. I was led to a beautiful female angel with almond-shaped eyes, wide cheekbones and long dark hair. She told me I was ready. This was quite something for me because over a long period of time I had been told again and again that I was to be patient, that it was a time of testing, a time of preparation, a time of healing. Just a few days earlier, during a previous shamanic journey, I had been told by my Lowerworld guide, a huge bird:

Stand up straight and feel the power within you. You
are filled with power. This is a time of preparation. You
must be steadfast in your trust and know that the
power is within you. This is a testing time. Know that
everything is being taken care of. Trust and keep faith.

He then began moving my arms up and down, back and
forth, as though I had wings, saying, 'Look, you are
powerful'. A smile spread over his face and he took me
flying. I asked, 'Is there anything I need to know?' And
he reiterated:

Know that this is a time of preparation and trust. The
power is within you. Stand tall and feel the power
within.

And now I was in the Upperworld and I was being told
I was ready. But what was I ready for? When I asked this
question I was shown a picture of myself writing books
about angels and running workshops introducing people to
angels. I also saw myself running workshops introducing
people to shamanic journeys. This was a huge surprise at
the time but these events have already come to pass.

I was then given a symbol in the form of a pale pink
rose. I was also given two pieces of quartz—one of rose
and the other clear—both in a beautiful pouch. I thanked
my guide, then, accompanied by an angelic entourage,
retraced my steps, slid down the rainbow and was back.

The next time I journeyed I was again taken to the
Upperworld, and this time I met an enlightened being who

has been my guide and teacher ever since. It was not immediately clear to me where I should go that day so I began by going to my special place, which feels as though it is somewhere *between* the worlds. I enjoyed the few quiet moments I spent there, sitting cross-legged on the thick grass looking out at the view below. Then I was met by two golden angels, each about eight feet tall, who took me by the hands and drew me straight through the clouds into the Upperworld. There again I was greeted by dozens of child angels, all excited to see me again. I asked the two angels who accompanied me who I was to meet. 'Will I meet my guide again?' (Expecting to see the beautiful female angel I'd met the previous time.)

Then suddenly, as though in response to my question, there was a surge of golden light before me. Instantly I was awestruck and overwhelmed with emotion. The light was everywhere. I could feel it pouring through me, filling me with love and warmth. I could feel it raining down on me, making my skin tingle. As far as I could see there was nothing but golden light.

Then, a face appeared in the light, came forward and, smiled at me, then receded and disappeared in the light. The face came forward again, smiling, then receding, subsumed in the warm golden light. He was in and out of it—showing his face but still being light, being all light and no longer a man, being all light then resolving into the face, then back to light. It was serious and playful at the same time. I was almost laughing I was so amazed. And the angels were all around—so happy for me. I was overawed but I also felt childishly joyful, as though I should be skipping around in circles, jumping up and down and clapping my hands. Then I felt a wonderful peace fall over

me and I said how pleased I was to be there with him and
to have him as my teacher. He said:

You are ready ... I am ready. I am ready to work
through you.

I was struck dumb with wonder. He then said:

The angels are waiting. It is time for them to come
down. People are desolate; they are in the dark. The
world is ready to move and it is time to bring the
angels down.

A week later, during a shamanic journey, a friend received
a message for me, which I taped. She said:

I could see a dark, cold, solitary landscape and I was
told, 'Cherie has spent time in the north. It was
deliberate. It was preparation. She had to learn to be
alone, and to learn the strength and wisdom that comes
with that. Often she thought she was just plodding
along but she wasn't. She was on our backs and we
were guiding her progress. But she is not there
anymore.'

She continued:

Then I was shown a sort of dating agency or
production line. There were dozens of people going
past and each time someone came in front of you, you

connected an angel to them, then the next person and another angel, the next person and another angel, and on and on.

It was as though you were sticking an angel onto everybody's shoulder. It was so funny. [laughs] There were streams of people—a bit like a production line—and you were matching each of them up with their angel. It was just lovely.

The imagery used by angels can often be humorous, as you have just seen, but it can also be poetic and extremely vivid. On one occasion, I did a shamanic journey for Morgaine who, feeling exhausted and overworked, was wondering whether the time was right to leave her job. The first thing I saw was a picture of her heart centre in the form of a fully opened rose. I was then transported to her workplace—a large office of relatively open space, some of it partitioned off into more private areas—and as I watched I could see that, wherever she went, she left a delicate trail of rose petals in her wake. Although some of her colleagues seemed oblivious to this, others were intrigued, and occasionally someone would even bend down and touch one of the petals and be instantly filled with light.

After telling Morgaine what I had seen, she felt certain that the message meant she should stay a little longer. Although she had dreams of her own to follow, she was sure that the time was not yet right to move on since her presence at work was still serving a positive purpose.

Some time later, Morgaine was again downhearted about her work situation. Even though she had always been willing to follow the guidance she received, being human, she, at times, found the path very tough going. I happened to call in to see her at work one day and as we hugged, her tears started flowing—she was almost at the end of her tether. I promised that as soon as I got home I'd do a shamanic journey to see if there was anything the angels wanted her to know.

As soon as the journey began I was taken to the Upperworld and there, waiting for me, was an angel wearing a pale blue robe. She had shoulder-length straight black hair, sparkling eyes, and very fine facial features. She was also carrying a sword. As soon as I saw the blue robe and the sword, the name Michael immediately came to mind. But this angel was by no means male, or even androgynous. As I puzzled over this the angel smiled enigmatically, and said, 'You can call me Michaela. I am the feminine face of Michael.'

I thanked her and then asked whether she had a message for Morgaine. She smiled again and as I watched she raised both arms to just above shoulder height. In her left hand she held aloft the unsheathed sword, and from the open palm of her right hand which faced in my direction I could see issuing dazzling beams of golden light. And the message? Michaela said, 'Know when to choose the sword, and when to choose the healing hand.'

In the highly-politicised daily reality of corporate life this was just the strong message Morgaine needed. And it came at exactly the right time.

# 4

# *Angel Timing*

## *At times of distress*

In 1997 I met Valda, an eighty-six-year-old woman, who had had many otherworldly experiences during her long life. One of the most vivid occurred at a time when, her children married and parents deceased, she decided to sell the family home and move away from the city to a house a good four hours' drive north, overlooking a little bay. As she said:

> I went there to live happily ever after . . . I hoped. But I moved into the house a bit too early—the electricity hadn't been connected, nor the telephone, and things were very unfinished and a bit uncomfortable. For the first time in my life I really knew what loneliness was.
>
> I was suddenly stricken with the dreadful realisation that I'd burnt my bridges behind me. I very much

regretted having sold my big old home, and very much regretted having moved up there. I was just a fool you see. I was warned not to do it, but, oh no, I *would* do it! And there I was, quite alone, because I'd left all my friends behind.

It must have been about three o'clock in the morning when it happened. I was very, very tearful and a little bit sleepy but I couldn't get off to sleep because I was too tragedy-stricken. And then I heard this *wonderful* voice booming right through the whole house saying, 'But you don't know how much sunlight is pouring into you!'

Oh, I *knew* it was an angel's voice. But even so I lit my candle and walked all around the house looking to see if anybody actually *was* bellowing through the window or something. But it was a high house on pedestals, and there was no-one there—nothing but snapping sticks and little sounds of night-owls and so on.

I knew it was an angel's voice. It was a male voice, a very strong voice, a reverberating voice that boomed throughout the whole house. It was reminding me that I have God's love within me, and to take courage.

From then on I was convinced that there are definitely angels around. I feel so grateful. I was very privileged.

Beth also expressed this same sense of gratitude after having had several experiences of her guardian angel at times of distress. She said:

I was at a stage where I didn't know how I was going to continue on. At that stage I really needed to know that there was someone there, that there was someone who was there for *me*.

I'd had contact with other beings of light but this was different. I believed in God, but somehow God seemed to be somewhat distant. When you're going through a lot of distress I think you do reach the stage where you say, 'I really don't know . . . If there *is* a God, what's he/she doing for me?' But by having my guardian angel appear to me the message was that someone really *was* there. And I really feel that that's what I needed to know—that there *was* someone there just for me. And I was so grateful.

Miranda felt the same way.

A couple of times in the last few years when I've felt distressed or worried I've just asked for help and straightaway I've felt wrapped in warmth. It's just gorgeous. So if anyone else is having trouble or having a really hard time I send that thought to them and ask *their* angel to wrap *them* up in warmth like that.

But the thing that had the most impact on me was the personalising of it—to be able to think of God or the angels as your father or your helpers. Not to think of them as distant beings. What I found was that they really care about you—you really do have a special angel waiting to guide you.

And Edward Hoffman reports the story of Eloise who, as a small child, was visited by 'two delightful beings' whenever she was distressed. These experiences had such an impact on Eloise that even many years later, aged in her seventies, she still remembered what a comfort their presence had been to her. She said she always felt these angelic beings with golden curly hair, blue eyes and fair complexions were 'a link to paradise'.[1]

## At times of deep questioning

Following a profound near-death experience when she was twenty-nine, Moira began questioning every aspect of her existence. Soon afterwards, during what she described as 'a very psychic phase', she moved into a flat with two girlfriends who were interested in spiritualism.

> I started going to spiritualist meetings with them. At first I pooh-poohed the whole thing but after a while I began to realise that there was something there that was inexplicable. I saw visions of angels ... beautiful beings ... and I felt I was getting direction from them. But I didn't say much about this at the time because I thought people'd think I was a bit of a crank.

In recent years Moira, now aged seventy-two, has been visited on several occasions by one particular angelic being. Some months ago she wrote to me:

> I now have a mighty Angelic Being—shining white— who appears to me in moments of deep pain or

questioning. Sometimes he is only partly visible, as
I believe he is too majestic to be seen all at once.
The name I receive inwardly is Angel Israel.

'Israel' means literally 'God strives' but spiritually
'Israel' means 'True children of God', or 'God
consciousness emerging from mental bondage'. I just
take it to mean that my spiritual understanding is
increasing and when my consciousness is truly spiritual
I will see him fully in all his shining glory.


And Valda, the eighty-six year-old woman, who was
suffering from intense loneliness, had another extraordinary
experience. She said:

It was about five o'clock one summer evening, and
I was sitting on my balcony overlooking a little
sheltered beach. I was wondering again why I had
moved up here leaving all my family and friends
behind, when suddenly I found myself standing on the
corner of the beach nearest to my house, in the shadow
of trees.

I saw, coming towards me, a beautiful figure looking
like pictures I had seen of Jesus. He wore a white robe
and a purply-blue cloak. His hair was darkish brown
and his eyes were penetrating and sad and a glorious
deep sea blue. He communicated a simple message to
me, which applied at the time, but his lips did not
move, nor did I hear the counsel with my physical ears.
Then, in a flash, I found myself sitting on my chair
again on the balcony.

Prior to this amazing but real episode I had not

really believed in Jesus. Coming from a more
Theosophical background I never took much notice of
the Christian insistence on Jesus. I never thought of
him as being more than just a fairy tale, another hope
established by man's idealism. So I never looked for
him.

But it wasn't the message that was as significant as
the *seeing*. The message saved me from possible disaster,
but that I *saw* drove the truth home like a rivet. Seeing
truly is believing.

And Melvin Morse reports the story of Dr Frank Oski,
a professor of paediatrics under whom he trained. Apparently Dr Oski, while still a medical student, had gone to
bed one night deeply disturbed about the fate of a dying
child he was treating, wondering why this child had to
die. Shortly after falling asleep he was awakened by a
brilliant light and saw at its centre the form of a young
woman with wings. This angelic being then proceeded to
explain to him why some children had to die. She revealed
to him secrets that she said most people only have revealed
to them when they die. 'Life', she said, is 'an endless cycle
of improvements.' Handicapped children often know this
and understand that their suffering will pass. Some 'have
even been given the challenge of teaching the rest of us
how to love'.[2]

This experience had such an effect on Oski that he was
always willing to share it with others, and he even wrote
about it in a major paediatric journal.[3]

## *At times of illness*

Cassandra Eason reports several cases of children who have seen angels. One, a ten-year-old girl, was sick in bed with the 'flu when she looked up and saw an angel 'in a long flowing gown with long flaxen hair'. She watched as the angel floated across the room in front of her and passed through the opposite wall, disappearing from sight.

Another sick child, a six-year-old girl, was looking out the window into the garden. Suddenly she saw 'a beautiful golden angel with wings'. She said she wasn't at all frightened but just lay there watching this wonderful being.[4]

And Edward Hoffman relates the story of a four-year-old girl who almost died after a measles innoculation. Apparently, for the entire duration of the child's illness there was 'a gentle lady in white' sitting by the side of her bed. Many years later, when talking with her mother about this illness she remarked on the presence of the 'kindly nurse', only to be told that there had been no nurse or any other person attending her. At that point she felt sure the wonderful being must have been her guardian angel.[5]

I have heard many people describe an angel who sat with them during a serious illness. Moira, who has suffered quite a lot of illness in recent years, told me that Angel Israel was always there for her whenever she was sick.

He always appeared when I was sick. And when I had this terrible trouble with my eyes ... I was just about despairing because I could no longer type, I could no longer read, I couldn't go on with the course I was doing, and I felt very, very trapped. And yet he came. And I had this wonderful feeling of blissful love.

I knew I was being loved and cared for. No matter what I was going through on this plane, he was there for me.

I once had a woman ask me if I could find out whether her nineteen-year-old grandson had an angel looking after him. She was upset because one side of his face had recently become paralysed. He was suffering from Bell's Palsy, an illness of unknown cause, which not only appears suddenly and inexplicably, as in this boy's case, but can disappear just as abruptly.

I did a shamanic journey and saw the young man's angel. She was very definitely female, of normal human size, with fair curly hair. And I could see that she was being very patient with him, and totally loving. I saw her just being with him, watching over and loving him.

She told me she saw him making a lot of mistakes in his life. And she was especially concerned by the way he followed along with the crowd and would not take responsibility for his actions. However, she made it very clear to me that whatever he did, however foolish it might be, she would still love him. Her love was unconditional and she would always be with him. But, she said, only when he realised he needed to take more responsibility for his actions would she be able to help him. She was adamant that he had to learn that lesson, and she would not intervene until he did.

A short time later I heard that the young man had begun to make a lot of positive changes in his life, and the paralysis had mysteriously left him.

In 1988 when I was interviewing people for my near-death experience study I met Stella, a tiny, fine-boned eighty-year-old, who reminded me of a sprightly little sparrow as she dashed about the room preparing tea and biscuits, chattering all the while. She lived in a nursing home and I spent an afternoon there with her. Apparently Stella had been close to death on numerous occasions and had had several experiences with angels. She said:

I was in hospital with this terrible illness—a bad 'flu and pneumonia. One night I had a turn for the worse and I heard the doctor say, 'Get the family.'

I think it was evening and I was lying there and I wasn't moving. Then suddenly everything was lovely. I didn't know I was sick anymore. And there was this angel in a white robe. It was so real, so beautiful. He was there . . . fresh looking. He put his right hand out and said, 'Hand of strength.' He didn't touch me, just looked at me. And the next thing I know, I'm all right. I was back. I was so sick at the time but then I got better.

When I got over this, not long after seeing this presence, one day I was lying there and I heard a voice say, 'Aah . . . aaah.' I half-opened my eyes and all around me were these dear little angelic beings, the size of little children, in flowing chiffon-like gowns. They were very tiny, darling little things. They were all leaning over the bed looking at me. I could hear their little voices saying, 'Aah . . . aah . . . aaah', like you do when ooh-ing and aah-ing over a baby.

I don't know why, but as I opened my eyes they all scattered. I could hear these dear little things moving—

whether they were floating in these gowns or whether they had feet I don't know. They rushed out of sight. I closed my eyes and they all came back again. I opened my eyes slightly and said, 'Don't go away. I'm alone. Don't go away.' But they fluttered away again. I could hear this rustling sound. It was most beautiful.

I don't know whether they were coming to take me away. I don't know. But it was very beautiful.

Some years later, one of my friends, a fellow near-death experiencer, told me of an experience she'd had during the illness of her daughter.

I was sitting by my daughter's bedside in a noisy, busy, public hospital ward. She had suffered a miscarriage and was bleeding heavily. And her blood pressure was dangerously low.

My mind went into blind panic and I could feel myself losing control. Struggling to calm myself I remembered reading an article about the angels and how we could call their names to ask for assistance. With great difficulty I stilled my mind and asked for help from the Archangel Michael.

Immediately I found myself saying to my daughter, in the tone of voice I used when she was a little girl, 'For goodness sake close your eyes and go to sleep!' And she did.

In a bustling ward, surrounded by people talking, she slept for thirty minutes. I watched as the colour gradually returned to her face and when she finally awoke, her blood pressure was normal and the bleeding had stopped.

I said a silent 'thank-you' to the Archangel Michael.


## At times of danger

In times of danger, angels make their presence known to us in many different ways. For instance, an angel may appear at a critical moment with an urgent message. George Gallup relates the story of a grandmother who was wakened during the night by an angel she described as 'bound up in light but with a human form'. This being didn't say anything but indicated that she should *immediately* check on her baby grandson who was sleeping in another room. After rushing to his side, she found to her horror that the glass bottle given to the child for the night had broken and the sharp end of a long sliver of glass was resting against the child's throat.[6]

Sometimes an invisible hand can be sufficient to avert danger, as in the case of a five-year-old child, who, ignoring the warnings of her parents, was heading into dangerous surf. Suddenly 'a gentle but firm hand' touched her shoulder, preventing her from going any further. Although there was nobody to be seen, the child sensed 'a calm presence' around her, and terrified, rushed back to where her parents were sitting.[7]

Isabelle, a seventy-eight-year-old woman, also experienced an invisible hand, but in her situation it was there to steady and prevent her from falling.

I was walking just after sunrise along a path by the sea.
I tripped, but instead of falling, I felt myself being

supported. I felt light and almost lifted. That may seem fanciful, but I felt light and supported until I regained my balance. I immediately thanked my angels who I knew must have been with me.

At that moment a man, who'd seen what happened, went by, and as he passed he said, 'I thought you were gone that time!'

Some people are aware of receiving support even without feeling the touch of an invisible hand. Mel was thirty-three years old when, as a field man with a geological exploration company, he was buried alive in a mine cave-in. He describes what happened:

I had a team of uni students with me down a mine collecting channel samples off the vein. I had gone ahead, and I'd gone up into a hole to clean off the face, when it caved in. So I was buried in there.

My first awareness was of numbness and extreme discomfort because I was down on the floor of the pit amongst all the broken rubble and stuff. My head was crouched well forward, my helmet pushed over my face, and I couldn't move except for my right hand. I knew I was damaged because there was that sort of icy cold pain through me. In actual fact, one arm had been severed, my back had been broken in three places, most of my ribs were broken, and one leg was very badly smashed up. I *knew* I was in serious trouble ... I was down there for twenty-three hours while they were trying to get me out.

At one point there was a movement in the rocks. Suddenly I was in a lot of pain, and then it was as though I passed out. Then I was looking back as though through a mist ... but with *such* compassion. It was like I was somebody else leaving that unfortunate creature down there, to go into some new path or new channel.

Then suddenly I could feel what was like a powerful surge, then a lot of pain, then something else slipped among the rocks and I had room to breathe again. And from then on there was a kind of peacefulness and a sense that it was all okay.

In visual terms, it was like there was a light beam holding me ... I saw no beings but there was certainly a consciousness that I had support. I certainly wasn't alone. Much of my peace was that there was something *much* bigger, *very* powerful, with me.

Dee also had the feeling that she was being looked after by an invisible force. She saw no beings, heard no voice and felt no touch but she was certain nonetheless that the angels must have been with her the day she crossed the desert. She said:

I was travelling across the desert in an old Renault and I had on board two children and a cat. And it was summer. It was the middle of the day but since the car had a problem with the carburettor, it often wouldn't fire up again after stopping, I didn't dare stop. But then I realised the petrol gauge was below empty. Well below empty!

I was thinking, 'I'll never make it to the next petrol station.' So while I was still driving along I tried to hail down any passing vehicle to say, 'Have you got any fuel for me?' I remember this lovely truck driver and he was in this enormous rig, and they're very high up. And he looked down out of his window at me and said, 'I'm sorry, girlie, I'm on diesel.'

So I kept driving and do you know I drove for three-quarters of an hour on below empty. Below empty! And I thought, 'This is not real. This is not how it usually is in my world.'

We eventually got to this funny little house with two petrol bowsers out front. Not a petrol station. And we literally coughed to a stop at the bowser. [laughs] And to this day I look back and I *know* I must have had help.

I have had many people tell me of angel experiences they had while out driving. In fact it was while at the wheel of her car, that Lisa first met Angel Raphael.

I knew angels were out there but the first time I heard Raphael's voice was one day when I was driving. There's a section of road coming towards home where you go up a hill and it goes over, and slopes, and goes down. I love it, it's like a big dipper. The speed limit's eighty kilometres and I do the eighty all the way up and over. It's wonderful.

Anyway, one day I was driving home and all of a sudden I heard a voice say, 'Slow down, red car coming across your path.' I automatically took my foot off the accelerator and started to brake. This was going *up* the hill. And as I got to the top and started going over, a red car was out of control and went straight across my path. If I'd been doing my normal speed we would've collided. And I was just like, 'Oh my God!'

I believed in angels but I didn't *believe* in them, if you know what I mean. I didn't believe that there was someone around me. But that was when I first heard Raphael's voice, and from then on it's like the gates were open and there he was.

## At times of pregnancy and childbirth

Miranda told me of many experiences she has had since the angels came into her life. And although she usually receives their messages through automatic writing, she was once given a remarkable insight into the world of her unborn child. She said:

The angels once gave me a really special gift. At the time I was pregnant with Emma and I didn't realise how cranky I was. You know how it is . . . During the night I was having to get up every few minutes to go to the toilet and I was getting more and more cranky. But then for about five seconds they let me tune in to where Emma was.

I've never had a near-death experience but in those moments I knew exactly what people who'd had a near-death experience were talking about. That pure love . . . without any worry in the world . . . and then, when you come back, how heavy it is!

I had been wondering if she was affected by my
cranky moods, but then I saw that she was totally
protected and surrounded by this *pure* love. And I
thought, 'Gosh, I'd better be nice to her when she
comes into the world, or she's going to get a terrible
shock.'

It was very special. But with experiences like this it's
something that's so real in the moment but afterwards
you've only got the memory of it.


Yet after talking with people about spiritual experiences
for more than a decade, one thing that strikes me again and
again is just how powerful these memories can be. Sixty
years after a near-death experience a person can still be
moved to tears as they relate what happened to them. Even
people who just read or hear about other people's memories
of spiritual experiences can be deeply affected. I have come
to believe that this is because it is more than just a story
to us, it is a *remembering* of an otherworldly reality that
we have all known at some time in the past. Other people's
experiences can ring true to us and be profoundly moving
since in a still place deep within us they are wonderfully
familiar.

Heather told me that the first time she ever heard of an
angel experience was fifty years ago, when she heard what
happened to her aunt during childbirth. Despite the passing
of time, this story has always stayed with her.

My aunt was giving birth to one of her seven children
when she almost died. Apparently she saw all these
beautiful angels coming towards her. And the feeling of

peace and joy that came with that vision she never forgot.

It may sound ordinary now but as an early teenager it's a story that really stayed with me, and as the years went by I could really see how that incident helped my aunt in later life to deal with one tragedy after another. Her eldest daughter died giving birth and left behind a husband and four children. Her second daughter died also giving birth and left a husband and one child. And it always amazed me how my aunt seemed able to accept this, and from outward appearances didn't experience a lot of grief with it.

In recent years I've thought it must have been her own experience of near-death that enabled her to accept losing those two daughters. And she's since lost a third daughter, and a grandson in an accident! She's now over a hundred—she had her hundred and fifth birthday in January—and on that day she said to me, 'This is the loveliest day of my life!' It's as though she has an inner joy and an acceptance of life no matter what happens.

Birth and death both are occasions for celebration and, I believe, are always attended by angels. Rosemary, who was present at the birth of her grandson, described what she saw:

I was there in the room just before he was born and I saw a ribbon of golden light with angels both sides. It was just beautiful! Just beautiful!

And remember Margot's account of the 'four pillars of divine light' that were present at the birth of her child.

> I never expected to see angels but then at the hospital they were so real! The four of them were so tall and so powerful!

Some time later, Margot had to have a hysterectomy.

> The night before the operation I cried and cried and cried. And again the presence came through. During that time of grieving I didn't see them but I could feel them there with me. And the next morning I was *so* calm.

## *For no apparent reason*

We have seen that people often meet angels at critical moments in their lives—at times of distress or worry, at times of spiritual crisis, illness or danger—but in some cases angels seem to appear for no obvious reason. For instance, Kelly said she was just walking in the mountains when she felt she was being lifted up by angels.

> It was quite strange because although I knew I was walking along, I felt as if I was being lifted up and being carried. It was a most wonderful feeling. It was a feeling of complete lightness, and excitement, and a feeling that I could do anything I really wanted to. It was a feeling of great joy and freedom. It was as if . . .

if I wanted to spread my arms out, I could even fly.
And I was aware there were quite a few of them there
with me.

And the first time seven-year-old Kayla saw an angel she
was simply lying in her bed. She was just three years old.
Initially Kayla was frightened but very quickly she realised
there was nothing to fear. She said:

She didn't have wings—angels don't have wings—but
she had lots of light around her. And she whispered in
my ear. I thought it was really nice.

And after, I saw tons of different angels. They all
looked very different, and there was one boy one. I
don't know what they say to me because I just hear
whispers. But I'm happy that they come.

I still see angels. I used to see them a lot but now I
just see them sometimes ... And sometimes when we
have meditation [at school] I see different ones.

About six years ago I received a letter from Betty, a
forty-seven-year-old woman, who described in vivid detail
an experience she had as a child.

I was five years old and wanted to go out to play. My
mother said not to go too far as it was going to rain. I
went and sat out on the kerb waiting for my friend to
come out and play with me.

I was playing with some pebbles when all of a
sudden there was some thunder. I looked up and in the

sky above the park across the road from my house I saw all these clouds. As I watched, they parted, and I saw a long stairway that went right up into the sky. I stood up and quickly started to go across the street towards it. Then, at the bottom of the stairs, I saw a misty figure. It turned towards me, and it was an angel. But it wasn't a lady or a man, not one or the other.

The angel looked right at me and put its arm out and beckoned me with its finger to come. I looked up the stairs and at the top was a bright light. It was beautiful and made me feel happy and excited. It was lovely and I felt so good. I started to run happily towards it but then I looked back.

I saw our house. I could see Mum and Dad and my sisters all bustling about getting dinner ready. And I knew that if I kept going I would never see them again. The choice was mine. I thought for a few seconds and then decided I wanted to go home. I wanted to go up the stairs with the angel too but I knew Mum and Dad would be sad. So I turned right around and ran home fast.

By the time I got across the road I was crying and yelling for my mother. I could hear thunder rolling and there was a lightning flash, so I ran inside. I told Mum what happened and she calmed me down and told me never to tell anyone of this as people wouldn't believe me. It was to be our secret.

Although, at first glance, it is not at all apparent why this angel appeared to Betty, many changes were to come about in her life which she attributes directly to this experience. To anyone acquainted with the after-effects of near-death experiences—no fear of death, belief in an afterlife, increase in psychic capabilities, little interest in material wealth, compassionate attitude to others, desire to help others, love of nature, et cetera—the changes she describes are very familiar. She writes:

After that, everyday life just went on but I used to have strange dreams and I could fly. I loved to go to bed at night because often I would rise out of my body and fly. I went to lots of places, across roofs and houses. I even saw where we moved many years later.

I suppose I became rather psychic but later I tried to repress these feelings. But then as I got older and had my own children it all came back again. Now I know and feel lots of things about people, and I see auras.

I love nature. I love trees and all creatures ... I feel we're all one with each other but that we just don't know it yet. And I love being in the bush. I work outdoors in a vineyard, and for seven weeks every year I pick apples. I love the orchard, I love the trees.

I also had the feeling I was special, here for a purpose. I knew I had to help people, be kind to people and animals.

I do not believe in material wealth. I only want what I need. I know we could all live a lot better if we didn't want things. Until I read your book[8] ... I did not know of any other person who had been through any of this. I did not know anyone else had had any of these feelings. I always thought I must be a bit strange.

I do not believe in religion, as such, but I feel a sort of spiritual love around me. I know the light I saw was

God and I will never be afraid to die. Ever since this
happened to me I've felt there was an angel watching
over me, a guardian angel. I know I am always watched
over and that I have the light always with me. I've felt
this from age five.

## Stairways to heaven

I was fascinated to read of Betty seeing a 'stairway that
went right up into the sky' since I have come across
numerous accounts containing similar stairway imagery.
For instance, paediatrician Melvin Morse and colleagues
reported the case of a fifteen-year-old boy who, after a
near-death experience due to cardiac arrest, told his parents
he had been climbing 'a staircase to heaven'.[9] And George
Gallup related the case of a seventeen-year-old girl who
had been seriously ill for three days following the birth of
her daughter. On the third day she had a near-death
experience during which she saw angels whose linked hands
formed a stairway that she ascended to heaven.[10]

There was Isabelle's vision, in which three angels clothed
in swirling golden gowns appeared to be descending a
staircase. And even Dionysius's celestial hierarchy is often
depicted as a staircase of angelic orders through which God
can reach down into human lives and human souls are able
to ascend to the celestial realms. But of course the best
known stairway to heaven is Jacob's ladder. In Genesis 28:
12 we are told that there was a ladder set up on the earth
which reached to heaven and as Jacob watched, he saw the
angels of God ascending and descending on it. Some scholars
make the point that this ladder image should not be taken

literally. For instance, in his interpretation of Jacob's famous dream ladder, the Rabbi of Kobrin believed that man was the ladder extending from earth to heaven. His view: 'Whether angels are going up or going down depends entirely on what man does.'[11]

From their dialogues with angels, Gitta Mallasz and her companions also learned that humans can be the bridge between earth and heaven. They were told that, as heaven descends through the levels to earth, humans need to be at the apex. Only at this metaphorical mountain peak is it possible for the two worlds to meet.

But just being there is not enough. Humans need to believe, for human belief forms an important strengthening strand in the bridge that allows angels to enter our world. If we are not ready, at the apex, believing, the feet of angels still have only emptiness beneath them. And even belief is not enough. Our actions must equal our faith. As the angels said:

> Only thus is balance on the peak possible. The one who stands high in the mountains needs a good sense of balance, *otherwise our feet step into emptiness.*
>
> Our being is drifting: beneath our feet we need the truth and the strength of the rock.[12]

The image of the ladder is also a popular theme in Sufi poetry. Indeed Mohammed's famous night journey (when he was carried to heaven on the back of the Buraq) is sometimes described as the mounting of a ladder or *mi'raj* into the sky. And apart from serving the purpose of establishing Mohammed's credentials, the so-called *mi'raj* stories also let people know what to expect when they die. In one retelling of the story, Mohammed even says that the *mi'raj* on which he mounted to heaven was the same one a dying man would see as he approached death.[13] What appears to us as death on earth is transformed into life in heavenly realms.

## Near-death experiences

Angels are very often associated with death and frequently appear during near-death experiences. Melvin Morse writes of a fourteen-year-old boy who had an NDE while hospitalised with a severe case of rheumatic fever. The boy related that while out of his body he became aware of the presence of two luminous beings, one either side of him. As he watched from above, the doctors tried to revive him, and all the while these angelic beings stayed close by his side. Eventually they gave him the choice of returning to his body or going on with them to the otherworld. He chose to stay and they left.[14]

Natalie, a fifteen year-old girl who suffered a life-threatening asthma attack, was interviewed by William Serdahely and reported a similar experience. During her NDE she found herself floating through a tunnel, hand-in-hand with two 'light figures'. Although she very much wanted to continue on into the world of light ahead of them she began to worry about how sad her family would be if she was to die. At that point the luminous figures released her and she returned to her body.[15]

Raymond Moody writes of Jason, an eleven-year-old boy who was hit by a car while riding his bicycle. During his NDE Jason found himself out of his body and travelling through a tunnel accompanied by two beings. He said he could 'feel love from them' but couldn't see them clearly until they all emerged into the light. At that point he said it was as though 'everything was lighted'. Moody also writes of a seven-year-old girl who hit her head when she slipped on ice. During her NDE she found herself in a wonderful 'garden' in the company of an extraordinarily beautiful loving presence.[16]

The light and love emanating from these beings can sometimes seem overwhelming and almost impossible to describe. In *Heading Toward Omega* Kenneth Ring reports the near-death experience of a man who nearly suffocated during an assault. As he approached the light at the end of the tunnel, this man described seeing 'a most beautiful being'.

> I have never, before or since, seen anything as beautiful, loving, and perfectly pleasant as this being. An immense love poured from it. An incredible light shone through every single pore of its face ... I was filled with an absolutely inexpressible amount of love.

Surrounding this magnificent presence were six 'shimmering' luminous forms. He continued:

> Their beauty, charm, splendid emanating colors, and the closeness I felt to them were breathtaking.[17]

In another of Morse's cases, a seven-year-old boy suffering severe muscular dystrophy, whose heart had stopped for three minutes, said that 'everything became dark, until I saw angels'. He described entering a beautiful world of light and although he chose to return to his body on that occasion, he died a few weeks later.[18]

In the vision of sixth century saint Salvius of Alby (recorded by Gregory of Tours in 590) once again we see the ascent of a soul accompanied by two angels:

> Four days ago, when the cell shook, and you saw me
> lifeless, I was taken by two angels and carried up to the
> height of heaven, and it was just as though I had
> beneath my feet not only the squalid earth, but also the
> sun and moon, the clouds and stars. Then I was
> brought through a gate that was brighter than our light,
> into a dwelling-place where the entire floor shone like
> gold and silver; there was an ineffable light and it was
> indescribably vast.[19]

Even Black Elk who, as a small boy had a near-death experience, described being escorted to the Upperworld by two beings. He was very sick, lying in his tepee with his mother and father at his bedside, when he saw two men 'coming from the clouds'. After calling to him they turned and 'left the ground like arrows slanting upward from the bow'. When Black Elk got up to follow, he noticed that he felt very light and was completely free of pain but when he looked back down he could see himself 'lying like the dead', his parents still by his side and he felt very sad to be leaving them behind.[20]

One of the people I interviewed for my near-death experience study, Patrick, had his NDE as a result of arthritic fever during World War II. He said:

> During my NDE I went through a tunnel. It seemed as
> though I was travelling very fast and there was a vague
> swooshing noise. It wasn't a continuous straight tunnel
> but a sort of winding affair, and I saw a light at the
> end. And I saw a wall. I imagined it was a brick wall
> but I couldn't tell you exactly. But people were going
> straight through it to the other side. They were just
> white shapeless forms but I knew they were people.
>
> I hadn't seen anybody till I got there, then they
> seemed to be passing me when I stopped. You know,
> they'd *sshhoooo* straight through the wall.
>
> While I was stopped there a voice said to me, 'If you
> go through like those people, you have to stay there.
> Make up your mind—if you go through, you stay.'
>
> I could see a golden light and I could see there was a
> city there brightly enveloped in this golden atmosphere.
> I couldn't say there were buildings there yet I *knew*
> there were buildings . . . There was no shadow . . . the
> light was all around. It was all enveloping. It was so
> perfect and I was in such perfect peace.
>
> I knew nobody there. I was completely on my own
> except for this wonderful presence. The voice was softly
> spoken and yet I felt it could reach into the universe.
> There was no question of shouting but the control was
> there. It was an all-embracing thing. This voice didn't
> seem to belong to anybody in particular but the light,
> I suppose, is part of it.
>
> And there was no time, time had gone. Eternity was
> there, there was no concept of time either backwards or
> forwards. I could encompass the whole lot, and I could

encompass the whole universe. This understanding was
the most amazing part.

Then the voice said to me, 'It's not your time yet.
You should really go back, but you can make up your
own mind. It's your choice.' So I thought of my father
and mother, and then I said, 'Well, I'm only twenty-
three, I've got a lot to do, so I'd prefer to go back.' He
said, 'The choice is yours.' And that was the end of it,
really.

Although my first thought was for my father and
mother I really felt I had to come back to do more for
my own development. I knew I hadn't completed what
I'd been sent here to do. Nevertheless when I first
found I was back I was disappointed. But then I was
glad that I'd been given a second chance, and I knew
that I'd be stronger for having had the experience.
From that time on I changed my whole life.

After the NDE I knew there was somebody or
something looking after and directing me.

Mary, a woman in her seventies who had her NDE
during an operation, described this post-NDE feeling in a
slightly different way.

I came back because I knew I hadn't finished what I'd
come to do. I wasn't told that but I knew. I remember
the light gradually becoming dimmer but it didn't leave
me inside. It's still with me. I can't remember coming
down a tunnel or anything like that. I just remember
the light becoming dimmer and then a gradual
awakening in a painful body. When I came to properly,

everything somehow seemed too hard, and yet a lot of that luminosity stayed with me. I still felt glowing inside.

## Death-bed visions

Angels also frequently appear in death-bed visions to the dying. These visions differ markedly from near-death experiences in a number of ways, the most obvious being that the person involved is conscious at the time of the experience, and observes the vision from the vantage point of, for example, the bed, rather than from out of the body.

Sir William Barrett, best known as the author of the classic book, *Death-Bed Visions* recorded an account provided to him by his wife. In her role as obstetric surgeon, Lady Barrett had had the opportunity of witnessing the experiences of a young woman who was dying of heart failure following the birth of her baby. At one point, despite being in a brightly-lit room the woman began complaining of increasing darkness. Then, as Lady Barrett recalled:

> Suddenly she looked eagerly towards one part of the room, a radiant smile illuminating her whole countenance. 'Oh, lovely, lovely,' she said. I asked, 'What is lovely?' 'What I *see*,' she replied in low, intense tones. 'What do you see?' 'Lovely brightness, wonderful beings.'[21]

Lady Barrett then commented on how difficult it was to describe the sense of reality that was conveyed by the woman's total absorption in this vision. Even the thought of leaving her newborn baby behind could not detain her on this side of life. The woman said, 'If you could see what I do, you would know I can't stay.'

In another case reported by Barrett, a ten-year-old child, Daisy, was dying. At one point she told her father that she could see 'so many' angels, and hear them singing, filling the room with their sound.[22] And a woman, Mrs. Z., who was very ill and close to death, was talking with her husband when she interrupted to ask if he could hear the voices singing. He couldn't. She then told him she'd heard them several times that day and felt sure they were the voices of angels 'welcoming [her] to heaven'.[23]

In 1996 I interviewed a seventeen-year-old girl, Angela, who had come close to dying, six months earlier, when she was hit in the temple with a hockey ball. She said:

> I was playing hockey. I'm a fullback and I was in a
> short corner set-up. A lady was having a shot at
> goal ... She had a shot at goal and the ball lifted
> and ... I can't remember any of this now but it hit me
> in the side of the head at the temple. And I became
> unconscious. From that I got a depressed fracture of the
> skull and parts of my skull cut part of my brain. I had
> a laceration on my brain and it smashed all the bones in
> my ear as well.
>
> I can't remember a lot of the time I was in hospital
> but they had to operate to lift my skull. And afterwards
> I was bedridden for two months. I was very close to
> dying.
>
> In the hospital (Mum was in the room with me) a
> group of angels came to me and wanted me to go with

them. There were probably about ten of them, just standing around, and it was really bright, not the sort of brightness where you have to squint, just very bright and very clear. The angels were all men, black and white men ... They were all really happy and [laughs] for some reason they really wanted me to go with them.

They were all wearing white ... I guess they were what you'd call traditional angels.

As it was happening I was actually talking to Mum about it. They were all saying, 'Come with me, come with me.' And I was saying, 'No way. I haven't finished what I have to do here.' And they were saying, 'Come with me. We want you with us.' And I said, 'No. I'm not coming with you. There are so many people here on earth that I want to be with. I haven't done what I'm meant to be here for.' And I was telling Mum this. So of course Mum got extremely scared thinking, 'This is it! She's going!'

They really wanted me to go with them. I could feel a pulling ... I was drawn towards them. It wasn't so strong that I couldn't pull away but it was strong enough for me to know what they were wanting. And they were all really joyous. In the end I said, 'No, please don't take me. Protect me but don't take me.'

Mum said the whole time I was talking with them she was just trying to be strong and call me back. So actually I think Mum brought me back. And then, they just left.

In 1977 Karlis Osis and Erlendur Haraldsson published the results of a wide-ranging survey into the death-bed visions of the dying, as observed by over one thousand doctors and nurses. Their findings showed that most of the apparitions seen by the dying were there to accompany them to the post-mortem world. As a typical example they report the case of a Pennsylvanian woman in her sixties. Although she had suffered a heart attack she was expected to make a full recovery and according to her doctor she was calm and not at all apprehensive. Then, at one point, looking towards the ceiling she said, 'I see an angel. He is coming for me.' After this episode she became even calmer, more serene than before and soon passed into unconsciousness. The next day she died.[24]

According to Osis and Haraldsson, many doctors expressed astonishment at the sight of a person dying following a death-bed vision despite having a positive medical prognosis. Another example is a ten-year-old girl who had been suffering from pneumonia. Apparently her temperature had dropped, the crisis had passed, and she was believed to be recovering. Suddenly the child's mother called for a nurse. The child had just told her that an angel had arrived and was taking her by the hand. At that point she died.[25]

Heather told me of a similar story related to her by a friend who had been present during the death-bed vision of her sister. Apparently, while sitting with her one day:

> Suddenly she just sat up off the pillow, stretched her hand out and said, 'Oh, the angels are coming for me!' Then she just lay back on the pillow and died.

Most dying patients take delight in the visions they see and are more than willing to go with their angelic visitors. But Osis and Haraldsson, whose study included a survey conducted in India, found that among the Indian cases a third of patients actually vigorously resisted the call to the other world.[26] This contrasted markedly with the American cases where only one person was unwilling to go.

Osis and Haraldsson suggested that this might be due to Indian mythology about Yamaraj, the king of death and his messengers, the Yamdoots. In a pattern similar to the western cases already outlined, it is believed that Yamdoots (the equivalents of angels) appear to the dying for the express purpose of taking them to meet Yamaraj. The difference lies in the outward appearance of the Yamdoots since it is believed that the karma of the dying person determines whether the Yamdoot will appear in benevolent or frightening guise. If someone has lived a good life they would expect to be met by a kindly Yamdoot but if they have strayed from the path they would know to expect a fearsome one. In these circumstances it is quite understandable for some patients to be terrified, and to frantically resist the dreadful prospect of being dragged away by a fierce Yamdoot.

Of course Indian culture is not alone in having a menacing image of death. As Osis and Haraldsson note, death has also been represented in western mythology as a frightening figure—the familiar scythe-wielding, black-cloaked, skeletal figure of the Grim Reaper. Yet it is clear that this image, as vivid as it is, could not be all that deeply imprinted on the western psyche since it did not appear once in the death-bed visions of the American patients.[27]

Despite the very different cultural conditioning between the two samples of dying patients, it was still clear
from the survey that the overwhelming majority of
Indian patients did not resist and fear the appearance of
the Yamdoots. On the contrary, most experienced very
*positive* emotions at the sight of their otherworldly death-
bed visitors. Indeed Osis and Haraldsson found that most
Indians 'light up' just as Americans do,[28] and they concluded that although after-death beliefs have some bearing
on the dying experiences of patients, they do not deter-
mine them. Even patients with no belief in life after death
or involvement with religion are seen to experience otherworldly visions of luminous beings in their dying
moments.

## Angel of death

The angel of death is a mysterious figure. There is little
agreement about who exactly the angel of death is, if
indeed it is one particular being. Azrael is often named,
and occasionally Sariel, and fallen angels such as Satan,
Sammael or Iblis are sometimes mentioned. Even Michael
in his role as psychopomp and Gabriel, as guardian of
the underworld, have been suggested. Metatron, who is
said daily to receive from God a list of souls to be taken
each day, is another. And, if causing death on a large
scale counts, that enigmatic being known as the angel of
the Lord is one more likely candidate. In 2 Kings 19:35
it is written:

That very night the angel of the Lord set out and
struck down one hundred eighty-five thousand in the

camp of the Assyrians; when morning dawned they
were all dead bodies.


## And to punish King David for his pride:

The Lord sent a pestilence on Israel; and seventy
thousand persons fell in Israel.
  And God sent an angel to Jerusalem to destroy it;
but when he was about to destroy it, the Lord took
note and relented concerning the calamity . . .
  David looked up and saw the angel of the Lord
standing between earth and heaven, and in his hand a
drawn sword stretched out over Jerusalem.[29]


The angel of death is not named in the Hebrew Bible
but in the Jewish tradition later writings suggest, among
others, Metatron, Azrael and Sammael for this role. It is
believed that Sammael's name may even be derived from
the Hebrew word *sam* for poison, which ties him in to one
of the most horrid images of death in this literature: an
angel standing at the head of a dying person, his sword
raised over the gasping mouth, a drop of poison falling
from its tip.[30]
  Although not specifically named in the Koran, in Islamic
lore the angel of death is Azrael. He is said to possess four
thousand wings and seventy thousand feet, and eyes and
tongues for every person in the world. It is said that every
time he blinks another person dies.[31]
  Abraham once asked Azrael how he could keep track of
all of humanity. How would he know which person to

take? Azrael explained that all human destinies are inscribed on the Preserved Tablet. And there is also the Tree of Life, which is covered with millions of tiny leaves. Whenever someone is born it sprouts a new leaf bearing the name of that person, and when a person is due to die his leaf begins to wilt and falls from the tree onto the Tablet.[32]

This story reminds me once again of the experience of Erin, the nine-year-old child who, during her near-death experience saw God as a wondrous being with 'all the heads of the whole galaxy'. While still in the presence of this being she had searched in vain for some sign of her own head. 'It must pop off when you die,' she concluded.[33]

Some people believe they can outwit or outrun the angel of death but there are numerous stories demonstrating how impossible this is. It is said that one day the angel of death entered the presence of King Solomon. He fixed one of Solomon's subjects with a fierce regard, then turned and left. The man was somewhat shaken when he learned who the visitor had been, and begged King Solomon to come to his aid by ordering the winds to carry him far away to India where he would be safe.

Solomon called on the angel of the winds with his six hundred and sixty wings to take the man to India. Shortly after, the angel of death returned and Solomon asked why he had been so interested in his subject. The angel replied that he was surprised to see him there since he had been ordered to take his soul from some place in India.[34]

For Christians, Archangel Michael is usually named as the benevolent angel of death who delivers the souls of the dead into everlasting life in heavenly realms. It is Michael who is said to have announced to the Virgin her impending death, and in Islamic lore he is known as 'the deliverer of the faithful'.

A deity closely associated with Michael is Hermes, called by the Greeks the Psychopomp or Conductor of Souls. He was similarly identified with Thoth in Egypt and Mercury in Rome. The Babylonian god of death is Mot and in Zoroastrianism the angel of death is Mairya. In the Viking age, in Scandinavia, one of the main cults was that of Odin, who was also equated with the Roman Mercury. It is said that he was worshipped by kings and warriors alike and that it was his spear that decided victory in battle. The valkyries the warrior angels of Norse legend, who as angels of death did his bidding, would fly over battlefields choosing who was to be slain and then conduct their souls to him in the halls of Valhalla, the Norse paradise.

In Hinduism, as already mentioned, the god of death is Yama, who, in earliest times was said to rule an afterlife realm not unlike Valhalla, where the deceased indulged in all kinds of carnal delight. It was in the post-Vedic period however that Yama was transformed into the forbidding personage so feared by some of the dying patients in Osis and Haraldsson's study.[35]

Sufi teacher Abdul Karim Jili tells us that the angel of death will manifest in whatever form is merited by the lives we have led. Those whose lives have been steeped in evil will be shown a cruel face but others can welcome his presence since they will be met by compassion and love. Indeed in the latter case Jili writes that when the soul sees the angel of death it 'falls in love' and is drawn gently from the body as though by a seduction.[36]

It is said that God wrote a message in letters of light on the palms of the angel of death, which read 'In the Name of God, Most Merciful, Most Beneficent'. Azrael was to show this message to any soul who was a 'Knower of God' and it would have the magical effect of drawing the soul out of the body like iron to a magnet or like light to its source.[37]

We have already seen the magnetic effect of the angels of death in most of the death-bed visions and near-death experiences outlined so far. And I know from my own near-death experience, which happened during the birth of Eden, how difficult it is to resist the glory, the joy and peace and the drawing power of the Light. Even thoughts of leaving my children behind barely gave me pause, and I have spoken with many other mothers who felt the same way. Of course all of those mothers *did* return to life, as I did, but for those of us who were given the choice, all agreed it was one of the most difficult ever made.

The Prophet asked Azrael how he took the souls of the dying and Azrael replied that at first he sent his angels, who carried with them the sweet smell of paradise. And as soon as the dying person sensed this perfume their soul began to rise. When it reached the throat Azrael would lift the soul 'with the greatest of care' and carry it aloft into 'the presence of its Lord'.[38]

Whenever a person dies, the angel of death is always

present. White Eagle teaches that, whatever the manner of passing, the soul is gently withdrawn and, enfolded in love, is borne away to begin its new life.

The Angel of Death is not a gruesome spectre as imagined, nor yet cold or cruel. Draw aside the veil of the Angel of Death, and you will see a face of ineffable mercy, pity and love revealed.[39]

# 5

# *Angel Roles*

AS HEAVEN DESCENDS, angels are our closest link to the celestial realms. They are here to awaken us to the divine— not only to a seemingly distant Godhead but also to the divinity everywhere surrounding and within our selves. As we bid them welcome, the angels also awaken us to our own potential, inspiring us to truly fulfill our divine purpose here on earth. Angels are emissaries from God guiding, advising, testing, teaching, watching over and warning, rescuing and healing. With angels in our lives miracles can and do happen.

Many of the people I've spoken with are sure that angels are appearing now for a reason. Rosemary said:

> I've been told that heaven must walk the face of the earth. I've been shown very clearly that this *will* happen if we really connect with angelic guidance.
>
> The vibration of their love and light will shift

previously held ideas, allowing more light to illumine a different reality, making it possible for high angelic messages to come into our hearts. And these angelic messages will bring guidance and definition, and a new perspective.

I've been told that it's essential that the choices we make in our lives do not come just from past patterns but rather emerge as a result of divine inspiration. And the angels have come to teach us this.

And Miranda said:

I think the [automatic] writings I receive are very special and I'm sure it's happening now to allow people to know that the angels are, more than ever before, drawing close to the earth. I don't know what's pending but they're saying something's pending and it's a time for everyone to listen.

## Angels as messengers

Angels carry messages but, as Miranda says, we need to hear and *listen* to what they are telling us. A few years ago a sequence of events began unfolding in my own life which illustrates well the importance of listening. At the time I was being told in my guidance that I was going to leave the city to live in the north of the state. I was very pleased about this but had no idea how or when this was going to come about.

I was patient for a while since I had already learned a major lesson about patience some years earlier and knew how important it was to allow events to occur in their own time. However, being human, every time I thought of leaving for the country I was anxious to get moving and do it.

That winter I was visiting my son, who lives in the same area I was to move to, and we were enjoying looking around at properties for sale. One day a photo in the local paper drew my attention—it was a rather blurry picture of a timber house set among rainforest trees—but as I was examining it more closely an inner voice said, 'This house is trouble!' And so it was to be.

On the last day of my holiday I was out driving with my son when he said, 'You know that house you saw in the paper is near here, would you like to ring the agent on the mobile and have a look at it?' I firmly refused: 'No, no, no, definitely not.' Then ten seconds later I picked up the mobile and arranged to meet the agent there. I couldn't resist.

It was a truly beautiful house on a few acres with a creek at the bottom of the garden. Everything I'd dreamed of. And it was affordable. I was very excited about it so as soon as I got back to Eden's house I did a shamanic journey to find out whether this was the place for me and was told that it wasn't. I could hardly believe it and was quite upset but somehow I managed to let it go from my mind. For a while.

The next day I flew home and as I walked into my small city apartment I felt as though I was being squashed back into a small black box. I was very unhappy and I began obsessing about the house again. In desperation I rang a friend who also works with angels and asked her what message she could get for me about the house. She immediately informed me it was not the right house. And she was also told that I needed to remember that it is just as easy to be pushed off 'the path' by something wonderful as it is to be waylaid by something negative. So I let go of all thoughts about the house once again.

Six months later I was at Eden's place again. This time I spent many pleasant hours in the car driving around familiarising myself with the area but I did not look at real estate, apart from finding out whether *the* house was still for sale. It was. During my forays into the hinterland, however, another place caught my eye—I couldn't see the house from the road but the long driveway, flanked by huge trees, was intriguing—and I contacted the agent to find out the price. It cost almost double the value of my apartment so I totally dismissed it as a possibility.

The months went by, and whenever I was unguarded I began obsessing about *the* house again. The angels must have been heartily sick of me by then but every time I asked I was quietly told the same thing. No. But one day I must have been pretty pathetic because the answer I received was much louder: '*This is not a punishment! It is the wrong time and it is the wrong house!*' At last I got the message and truly let go of my obsession. It was wonderful, I felt I could breathe again, and for the next six months my life was most enjoyable. I truly was living one day at a time and to my amazement I even found pleasure in being in the city again. During that extraordinary time I met several new people who are now an important part of my life, and began another important phase of my work.

Over the summer holidays I was again at Eden's place. This time I was adamant that I would not look at, or even think about, real estate. I was having a wonderfully relaxing holiday when one day, while out driving, I noticed we were approaching the street where the beautiful driveway was, so I suggested we drive up there to have another look. I was astonished to see the property was still for sale. We decided, just for fun, to make an appointment to see what sort of house was at the end of that driveway.

Two days later we went along and I immediately felt I'd come home. This was my house. But how could this be? It was far too expensive.

As it turned out, the owners had, just that week, dropped the price by a considerable margin. And, in the intervening eighteen months since the saga of 'the house' had begun, my apartment had almost doubled in value—the result of a sudden real estate boom. The miracle was that now I *could* afford this house.

That night I tossed and turned, worried that again I would be told this was not the house for me. At about 3:00 am I asked the angels what I should do and was told that this *was* my house. I was also told not to worry, everything would go as smoothly as a bird's flight. And it did.

I have been living here now for eighteen months and I am constantly filled with wonder and gratitude. Had I not weathered the testing, had I not listened to the angelic messages I received, I know I would not be here today.

The other house sold soon after. It was as though it had been used as a decoy to seduce and torment me, to test the strength of my patience and willingness to trust. And, needless to say, this was not the only area of my life being tested at that time. Life is complex and there is a lot to learn. Some lessons are inevitably tougher than others but I have come to understand that if we remain steadfast and are true to the guidance we receive, the spiritual rewards are infinite.

And of course the messages we receive are not only about spiritual growth, patience, trust, et cetera, they also have a purpose in the physical world. Rosemary related a simple episode that happened to her just the day before we spoke. She said:

> Yesterday I got a message from Gabriel. I was told, 'Stay put!' I wanted to go out but I was told, 'Stay put!' And I thought, 'But I don't want to stay put and stay home by myself.' It was Sunday night about five o'clock. I had no television and I didn't feel like just sitting here. I wasn't expecting anybody but I was being told, 'Stay put!'
>
> As it turned out, that evening two people unexpectedly came to visit me. I introduced them and it was very important for them to be introduced.

And Diana had an odd sort of experience that ended up being quite important for her. She said:

> Many years ago I'd done a lot of reading of Dawn Hill. Then one day recently I was just walking upstairs when I heard something like a trumpet sound, then a voice calling 'Dawn Hill!'
>
> I was pretty shocked and I thought, 'Dawn Hill?' I called out to my husband, 'Did you hear that?' And he said, 'Hear what?' And I said, 'That noise and then Dawn Hill!' And he said, 'No, no, I didn't hear it.'
>
> I went and lay down and I was thinking, 'Dawn

Hill?' And then it came to me: the books! Obviously I was being told to go and look at them. And I thought, 'I'd better take note of that message—it was so loud!' But then I thought, 'Gosh, you don't have to shout!'

When I went back to those books I found all sorts of things in them that explained what had been happening to me. It helped me a lot.

And Olivia received a prophetic message.

After receiving that message I could see where I was heading in life. I could see certain things were going to happen. They weren't things that I was particularly pleased about at the time, but I could see it all very clearly and I knew what I had to do, so a whole big load that I'd been carrying around for ages was lifted. It took something like three-and-a-half years for it all to work out, but since I knew where I was heading I didn't have to worry too much.

Kenneth Ring quotes a letter from Ann who had a near-death experience during childbirth. While in the otherworld Ann was met by a being of light, who told her she had to go back to her body but that four days later he would come to collect her baby. On the second day of her life, Ann's daughter had a cerebral haemorrhage and two days later she died. While everyone around her was devastated by the news, Ann's time in the world of light had been such a positive experience for her that she could only feel joy for her daughter.[1]

As we've already seen, many people hear angelic messages around the time of death. For instance, William Serdahely tells the story of Karen, whose great-grandmother was dying and was very distressed that her affairs were not in order. But then an angel apparently appeared to this woman telling her not to worry, and reassuring her that everything would be all right. And the next day she died.[2]

Reassuring messages may even come through *after* death. We have already seen how angels, as divine messengers, are sent to conduct the souls of the dead into the otherworld but at times they may even accompany them back. In my book, *Beloved Visitors*, there were many stories told to me by parents whose children had died. All of these parents had been comforted at some point by a visitation from their deceased child.

Shortly after *Beloved Visitors* was published I received a letter from Alvia, who told me of a remarkable episode that occurred a week after the death of her son, Bill. In Alvia's experience, her son returned accompanied by an angel. She wrote:

My son, Bill, died in a road accident on 13 April 1997. I had my experience a week later on Sunday 20 April. The night before, I had said to God, 'Oh Lord, why couldn't Billy say goodbye?'

At 4.30 am I was awakened by somebody embracing me very firmly with their hands digging deep below my shoulder blades. I seemed to awaken into a state of greater awareness and saw Bill bending over me. The area of his face around the nose, mouth and chin was illumined by a soft light and I saw their contours exactly.

I threw my arms around him and cried, 'Bill, Bill, my beautiful boy! Blessed be the name of the Lord!' (I was praising God for sending him to say goodbye.)

Then Bill kissed me fervently on the lips, pressing my lips against my teeth. The kiss seemed to last about two minutes. As I embraced Bill I could feel the muscles in his back flexing, and the clothing he wore seemed to be almost part of his skin. He seemed as solid as you or me.

There was an angel with him. I could not see the angel but sensed he was there. Then I felt the vibrations of the angel's hand below mine patting Bill on the right back waist area as if to say, 'Come now'. Then they were gone.

It is easy to imagine just how reassuring such a visit would be. Kim had a similar visit following the drowning of her three-year-old son William. She was lying in bed on the day of the funeral, exhausted, not sleeping, not meditating, with eyes closed. Suddenly William was there with her.

When he was alive he hardly ever talked, you know, even though he was three he didn't talk very much, but when I was with him after he passed over he was talking to me like anything. [laughs] He was just telling me all about it, what had happened. It was a long conversation. I've sort of got it still in here but I can't remember all of it. He told me that he loved us and that he was only here for a short while. He was there with me and he was just sort of saying that it was his time and all of that. He was talking to me because I still couldn't believe that it had happened.

My grandfather was there too. After the drowning I kept seeing my grandfather holding William, and I kept rejecting that image because my grandfather had passed over about three years before that. But all the time I could see him holding him ... Anyway, after a while, I don't know how long this went on for, but my spirit guide came to me. I used to see my spirit guide as a being of light. He said to me, 'It's time for William to go.' And I said, 'No, I don't want him to go.' And I said, 'No, I can't let him go.' And I just sort of held on to him. And this being of light said, 'It's time for him to go', and I said, 'No, I can't let him go.' Then he changed into a human, an ordinary man I could see. And he was very gentle and he very compassionately said, 'It's time, it's time.' And I said, 'No, no I can't.'

Just in front of us there was a golden light, an arc of light, brilliant and gold, and there was all this peace. And then out through the light, the first thing I noticed were a pair of bare feet, and then the white robe, and it was Jesus coming out through the light. I'll never forget it. He came out to me, looked straight into my eyes, and he said, 'My child, it's now time to take your child.' So, I said, 'Okay.' And I gave William to him. No worries. I guess, like, I know Jesus. It was an incredible feeling. And then he just turned around and he had him. I can't remember whether he was holding him or was walking with him. I can't remember that bit now. But they all just went back—my grandfather, my guide—they all went back through the light. And as they were going back I heard angels, I heard music.

I saw angels, the angels were above the arc of light.
And I was thinking to myself, 'Am I dreaming this?'
I opened my eyes then I closed my eyes straight
away and I was still there. It was an incredible
feeling.

I think I was very privileged to be able to see that. If
only other mothers or other parents could go through
that experience too. It gave me so much comfort. I
haven't told a lot of people about it but to me it was
more real than anything on this earth. It was really
incredible.[3]

Although a direct spontaneous experience such as this is
one of the greatest gifts bestowed by angels, there are other
means of receiving messages. One is the use of oracle cards
such as Tarot cards or angel cards, and another is the use
of a chart such as the one in Jane Howard's book, *Commune
with the Angels*.[4]

Howard's chart is titled 'The twelve rays of God's
consciousness' and provides a wonderful focus for meditation. She believes that the angels today are encouraging
us to awaken to our true identity as children of God,
'composed of all twelve aspects of the God Presence.'[5] For
each of the twelve rays on the chart there is a key word, a
colour, an archangel and archaii, a divine attribute and a
seed thought. Howard suggests that we should read the
chart carefully then, after quieting the mind, ask the angels
to direct us to the ray we need to begin with. She then
suggests concentrating on that particular ray until there is
a sense of completion. Days, weeks or months might pass
before it feels right to move on to another.

Isabelle told me of her experiences with this chart.

I had had the book for a couple of years then one day, when I was particularly upset, my daughter suggested I re-read it. Strangely enough it had fallen from the bookshelf just a couple of days before.

When I returned home I took the book out and, asking for a message, I let it fall open. It opened at a page which told me I should pour my heart out to the angels and ask them for divine guidance in resolving my problems. This was exactly what I needed to hear at the time. So since then I've read it regularly.

When I first saw the chart listing the archangels and archaii, the colour that first attracted me was gold. I soon found out that it represented Archangel Valeoel and Archaii Peace. And the divine attributes associated with them were peace, comfort, inner calm and balance.

Each morning on my early morning walk, I give thanks for all my gifts and blessings. And I meditate and pray and ask the help of my angels. So while I was meditating on that ray I was calling on Valeoel and the archaii for help in my daily life.

Then, after a week or so, Hope kept entering my mind. I looked back at the chart and found that Gabriel and Hope were together and their divine attributes were purity, hope, resurrection and ascension. When I read this I was sure I was being guided because I had been praying to make my heart pure and 'to make the earthly part of me wholly Thine'. (This is the essence of a hymn which I say to myself during my walk.)

Then, some days later, Michael and Faith kept entering my mind. And when I looked at the chart I found them to be angels representing God's will and giving me faith, power, protection and order ...

By focussing such attention on the angels through this sort of practice Isabelle found that her daily life became filled with synchronicities and angelic messages. One particular message came in the form of a teaching and had a powerful effect on her.

A few days later, while on my walk, I was asking for help to overcome some unhappy hurts that were making me feel quite bitter. I was trying to think of them, one by one, letting myself feel the hurt again. Then I heard the angels tell me, 'That's right. Experience it again and then let it go, and *forgive* and *forget* as you would have others forget the hurts that you must have dealt them throughout your life.'

This struck me like a blow but instantly I knew I was freed from the bitterness, and I was thankful.

A few days later I was meditating during an acupuncture session and I kept seeing and sort of sensing the colour amethyst. I couldn't think what it represented but when I got home I looked at the chart.

As I read through the chart I became so excited because, although the closest colour was violet, the archangel and archaii were Zadkiel and *Holy Amethyst* and the divine attributes were *freedom, forgiveness, mercy* and *compassion*.

It's become so commonplace to me now that I don't even think about it. I've only *seen* angels once since my first experience with the three angels but I always feel

that I have angels with me. I don't know how. I just
know they are there. I can ask them to let me know
that they are present and I feel a cool breath or
flurry . . . just cool energy, perhaps on my cheek . . . I
can feel it now.

## Angels as teachers

Isabelle's most powerful angel experience took the form of
a session of supervised learning, during which she was
taught a lesson that has had a profound effect on her life.
You might remember her description, in a previous chapter,
of the three angels who appeared to her on that occasion.
They were positioned, one above the other, as though
descending a stairway, and wore buttercup-coloured diaphanous gowns. Isabelle suddenly found herself out of her
body, alongside the angels, watching herself as she sat on the
bed with her knees pulled up, her arms clasped tightly
around her legs and her head resting on her knees. She said:

I could see that the little creature down there, who I
knew to be me, was filled—jammed full right through
her torso and up into her head—with these dark balls. I
believe they were dark, misshapen balls of negativity
and they were dark and misshapen because so many of
them had been jammed in on top of each other. I just
*knew* that it was negativity, and I also knew I had to
get rid of it myself. I knew I couldn't just remove it by
breathing in the breath of God and saying, 'Go.' It
needed more than that. And all in the same instant I
knew that it was negativity somehow related to my
mother, my husband and my sister. Then, while I was

watching, one popped out, and it was my mother. I could see her hair and her glasses. And I could see her face—not clearly—but I could see enough to know it was her.

That was the first time the angels came to me. It was wonderful having them there because I knew they were a manifestation of God, and that they were there to show me what I needed to do. I'd been asking, because I'm always asking for help with one thing or another, and at that time—it's three years ago now—I was always asking about what I should do ... I was terrified of hurting these people that I loved so dearly.

And when that ball of negativity came out, and it was my mother, I remember really crying and telling her how much I loved her. You see I always wanted to do *everything* for her myself and I was always being censured by everybody—my husband, my sister, my children—for doing that. But at that moment, for the first time, I realised *why* I'd always wanted to do everything for her myself: so she would think I was ... good. But I never did quite measure up. Nothing was ever quite good enough.

I suppose I'd always wanted to be all things to all people. It's such a cliché ... but I honestly did want to help. But it was made clear to me, and I don't really know how, but it was made clear to me that if I really wanted to help, first of all I had to be myself. But there I was down there all clotted up with my head in my hands. I didn't know *who* I was—I was so jammed full of negativity.

But that day I *knew*, and I don't know how the

angels did that, but I *knew* I had to remove that negativity myself. It wasn't put in words like that but I *knew* then what I had to do. I have now become stronger and much more of a person in my own right. And I have begun to do things and be more independent, without being so afraid of hurting my sister or my husband. That experience has really meant everything to me. It has changed my life. It's totally changed my way of thinking.

What I learned was that by attaching myself to these people to help them, I was *not* helping them because *they* have to live *their* life in *their* way, otherwise they're not doing it properly. And if I'm so attached to them I'm not doing my own life properly either.

It's all had such an impact. It's changed my relationship with my husband and my sister very much for the better. I feel freer with them. I no longer feel that what *they* think has to be what *I* think. I don't feel so attached. I don't love them less, but I don't feel so attached.

And that was a very significant change for me. But it was a blow in a way too because I felt, in a way, so wasted. There I was, seventy-five years old, and I'd wasted so much time . . . Now I look ahead to the future with great excitement. It's really opening up for me. It's wonderful.

Isabelle made the point that she was always asking for help, so we should not be surprised that she received it. However, many of us forget to ask. Olivia said:

My biggest lesson has been to ask the angels for help.
I'm always telling other people to do it, and I really
mean it but I forget to do it for myself. It's not that
I'm trying to be a hero, I just don't think to do it. It's
really silly.

Beth maintained that the greatest lesson she learned from
the angels was that they are always there for us.

All I have to do is say I'm in need and my angel is
there for me. I don't even have to say what the problem
is. I don't have to talk and say, 'I've got all these
problems'. All I have to do is say 'I'm in need' and he's
there. When I'm in need he's in front of me, the rest of
the time he's behind me but what I've learned is that
he's *always* there.

Lisa told me that in the teachings she receives from Angel
Raphael he sometimes makes an important point about
timing.

I was always being told that some thing or other would
come into my life *when the time is right*. That's one of
his big things: timing. He generally tends to emphasise
the present. You know, 'take care of now', don't worry
about what's going to happen in five weeks time or five
days time or five hours time, because unless you deal
with *now* everything is going to change anyway. You
can't go from point *A* to point *B* unless you take it one
step at a time. If you leave one out, if you don't do

step number three or four, you're going to end up
somewhere else. I was always being told, 'Don't worry
about it. It will happen. There's no use having it now if
you aren't ready for it.' And what I learned is that if I
rushed things, tried to take a short cut or left out a
step, the outcome would always be wrong.

Despite an occasional short detour for this sort of lesson,
according to Lisa, Angel Raphael's teachings usually
remained focussed on trust and love. She said:

In the early writings everything was 'Trust', 'trust',
'trust'. And I'd think, 'Hm, there's a certain theme
here!' [laughs] And there's a lot about looking within
and healing as well as trusting. And loving. The message
is simple. People scoff at it because it is *so* simple.
Messages like 'Look within' and 'Trust yourself', 'Look
in your heart'. They are such simple messages that
people go, 'Bah, humbug!' 'Forget it!' That sort of
thing. But once you look within, you see yourself in a
new way. And if you can accept yourself you can
accept others. He talks a lot about tolerance of other
people and other ways.

Kenneth Ring relates the story of Jayne, who had a near-
death experience while in childbirth. During her experience
she encountered a being of light, who asked her the same
question: 'What is in your heart?' She found that somehow
she was able to look within, and what she found there was
nothing but love.[6]

And in another of Ring's cases, Harold, who had an NDE as a result of a post-operative haemorrhage, described being met by a 'brilliant white-yellow warm pillar of light'. While still immersed in the warmth and love of this encounter, he was asked what he had done to benefit the human race. He then watched his whole life pass before his eyes and saw very clearly that the things he'd thought were important counted for nothing and, 'what I counted in life as unimportant was my salvation'.[7] And Darryl, who had his NDE when lightning hit his house, also had a life review in the presence of a supremely loving luminous being. As he watched the review, seeing the effect he'd had on other people, he was shocked to find what a 'terrible job' he'd done in his life. As he said, 'Lookin' at yourself from the point of how much love you have spread to other people is devastating.'[8]

Shana is a near-death experiencer I first interviewed in the late eighties. I later included her story in my second book, *Within the Light*, and I've never forgotten her description of the love she found in the other world, and her clear understanding that as a result of that experience she was on earth for one reason only: to lead a life of service.[9] She said:

I was in hospital for a very simple kidney operation, but I went into shock because of an allergic reaction ... I had three cardiac arrests, all from shock. And I saw a whole movie of my life—everything. It was incredible. I remember at the time being amazed at the things that I'd forgotten. I saw everything from day one right up to the present day, every single little thing. I didn't feel judged at all—it was fantastic. It was like I was watching this movie of my life, it was fascinating.

That was great, but then I had the feeling of all my senses closing down, just the whole body, shutting down. It was very weird. And then I was outside my body, and I was watching everybody working on me . . . [and] I could see everybody I was connected to. It was just one big global thing. And there was this incredible feeling of compassion that I'd never felt before.

And while I was up there it was like I was in this golden world, this incredible golden world filled with Christ's light. I just felt I was part of it all, part of the whole, that this was where I belonged, that this was the truth. And there were all these beings, angels, angelic, luminous beings and this feeling of *total* love. And the one thing I got when I was up there was that my task was to serve, that the only purpose for humans is to serve the planet and to live life absolutely to the fullest. I knew that was the way to get back there . . . My path was to come back here and to serve.

I was only twenty-three . . . So it took me quite a while for everything to come together—to get used to the fact that I was back, to work out what the message was, to realise what it meant to say my life was to be of service.

At first I went through a self-denial stage—you know, like everything that I had, I had to give away. I thought that I shouldn't have anything. But eventually I worked out that that wasn't service, because it made me very rigid. And I went through a lot of other things until I eventually came to know that service was, for me, to understand myself—I first had to love myself before I could love others.

According to Morris Margolies it is said that while still in the mother's womb every child is taught all the wisdom of the Torah by an angel. But, just before birth, another angel comes along and causes the child to forget it all again. Why would one angel give knowledge if another is going to erase it? What is the point? Rabbi Baruch of Medzibozh maintains that, despite the best efforts of the angel of forgetfulness, some vestige of these teachings would always remain imprinted on the child's mind. The challenge in all of our lives then, according to Rabbi Baruch, is to bring this knowledge to the fore, 'allowing the teaching angel to have the last word'.[10]

## Angels as guides

In one of his fairy tales, Hans Christian Andersen wrote:

> Every time a child dies, an angel of the Lord comes
> down to earth, takes the dead child in his arms, spreads
> his large white wings and flies to all the places the child
> had loved. He then picks a posy of flowers and takes
> them to God, so that they may bloom there even more
> beautifully than on earth. The good God takes the
> flowers to his heart, kisses the one that is dearest of all
> to him, and this one is granted a voice and allowed to
> sing in the choir of the blessed.[11]

The angel acting as psychopomp, guiding the soul to the other world after death is by now a familiar image. It is very common to come across near-death experiencers who relate that they were accompanied to heaven by one or more luminous beings. Genevieve, a nine-year-old child I interviewed, said:

> Two angels came to get me and I didn't know their names because I didn't ask. And when I got to heaven I saw people moving around and I figured out they were angels because I saw their wings. And I saw gold and silver, with trees and flowers all around.
>
> Then I saw Jesus and I said I wanted to come back and he said, 'Yes. It is not your time.' And then the same angels brought me back to earth.

Some people are given a guided tour of sorts before returning to their bodies. Beverly, a near-death experiencer, who wrote out a version of her NDE for Kenneth Ring, related that she was taken by the hand by 'a radiant being bathed in a shimmering glow' and taken upwards into the world of light. There she found herself in the presence of the supreme Being of Light, who she called God. Before being returned to her body, Beverly was taken on a 'voyage through the universe' and was shown countless 'celestial events' such as the birth of stars and exploding supernovas.[12]

Beverly's story reminds me of Jung's near-death experience, which he described in some detail in his autobiography, *Memories, Dreams, Reflections.* In 1944 Jung had a heart attack and as he hung between life and death he found himself high up in space.

> Far below I saw the globe of the earth, bathed in a gloriously blue light. I saw the deep blue sea and the

continents ... My field of vision did not include the whole earth, but its global shape was plainly distinguishable and its outlines shone with a silvery gleam through that wonderful blue light.

Jung's attention was then drawn to a gigantic, 'dark block of stone, like a meteorite' that was hollowed out to form a temple. At its entrance sat a Hindu wearing a white robe and Jung knew he was expected. He wrote:

As I approached the temple I had the certainty that I was about to enter an illuminated room and would meet there all those people to whom I belong in reality ... There I would meet the people who knew the answer to my question about what had been before and what would come after.

But before he could enter the temple, Jung was told he had to return to his body. 'Profoundly disappointed', it took him a good three weeks before he could make up his mind to live again. However, once recovered, he began one of his most fruitful periods of work.

It was only after the illness that I understood how important it is to affirm one's own destiny. In this way we forge an ego that does not break down when incomprehensible things happen; an ego that endures, that endures the truth, and that is capable of coping with the world and with fate.[13]

Another near-death experiencer, Bob, also began his near-death experience by 'hurtling through the universe' through a tunnel of planets. But after arriving in the other world he found himself in the presence of a radiant being who 'wore a white robe and exuded peace'. For a while they sat quietly side by side overlooking a beautiful landscape but then Bob's angelic companion suggested they should be on their way.

The tour began with a stop on a beautiful street, where Bob marvelled at the joyful attitude of the street-sweeper. He then found himself watching a choir of angels singing the most extraordinary music he had ever heard. Then suddenly he was in an art gallery filled with indescribably beautiful works of sculpture and painting. Next, he materialised in a computer room, which, he said, 'was a place of great activity, yet peace prevailed.' There he was encouraged by Albert Einstein to operate a computer which 'guided the path of destinies'. A library was the next port of call and there his guide directed him to learn from the wisdom of all ages that was before him.

At this point Bob became anxious about returning to his body. He was appalled at the thought of having to return to his dreadful life after experiencing such bliss. His guide then performed the remarkable feat of healing the painful areas of his life, replacing pain with 'a glorious sense of wellbeing and love'. Shortly afterwards Bob found himself in the recovery room, and as he said, 'The effect of the experience on my life was immediate and electrifying.'[14]

Hal was also taken on a guided tour. He was fourteen years old when he had his near-death experience as a result of heart failure.

After travelling at immense speed through a dark tunnel

for a very long time Hal eventually tumbled out into a beautiful landscape where he was met by two boys, one of whom he'd known at school. This boy, Edward, had drowned three or four years earlier. Edward accompanied Hal as he explored various aspects of the new world around him—meeting deceased relatives, asking questions, receiving information—but then Edward told him that he now had to meet the Light. Hal said:

> I could see in the distance a pinpoint of light and it was coming towards me . . . It seemed to be coming from hundreds of miles away, and it was coming at immense speed and it just kept getting bigger and brighter . . . As the Light got closer the feelings of peace became even greater. It was a wondrous feeling.
>
> The Light came up to me and he spoke. I must have talked backwards and forwards to the Light for quite some time, perhaps as long as half an hour. Then our conversation sort of petered out and the Light had to go off somewhere.
>
> They gave me a choice then. I could do one of two things—either I could go over and have a look at the city or I could go into a big building which was the archives. I chose to go in there.
>
> When we went into the archives we seemed to bend down to go into it. We went first into a big room and there were people on the right seated at a table. They looked as if they were in conference, they didn't take any notice of me . . . We then started to walk along a corridor that was immediately in front of us. It seemed to be only about twenty feet in length, but as we went into it, we kept on going and going and going. It seems

to me that perhaps we went a mile. It was a *long* walk.
There was Edward and the other boy and myself and I
think there were other people with us but I'm not too
sure.

As we were going along there were corridors
branched off to the left and right. And the room, this
corridor, was alive. It was living, it was a living room.
It had walls going up to about ten feet, and then the
next section of the walls sloped in, probably came in at
an angle of about fifteen degrees, and above that was
the ceiling. I can't recall what the ceiling looked like.
But those upper wall panels that were leaning in
towards us seemed to be beaming knowledge to me.
And as I went through, all this knowledge was coming
to me, and history was resolving itself. And everything
that was known to mankind was in these archives and
was coming down into my mind. And by the time I got
to the end I knew everything. I knew all that had ever
happened. But I can't remember any of it!

Eventually we did get to the end of the corridor, the
corridor ended and there were picture windows at the
end and I could look out and look into the city because
this building extended right up to the city. When I
looked out there were people there and they were
moving around ... We turned around then and came
away.

When we got back to the doorway and ready to
leave the building Edward said to me, 'Well, I'm going
to take all this knowledge away from you now.' He
said, 'You're not allowed to take that back.'

After that we went out the door ... [and] back to
where I'd come in ... Then he said, 'Right-o, it's time

to go back now ... It's nothing to worry about, you just step out, it's like stepping out of a bubble. And you'll see your body as soon as you get out.'

His last words to me as I was going through were, 'When you get back in your body, whatever you do, breathe. You've got to breathe. Now remember that.' ... Anyway I got myself back into my body and then I started to breathe.

Then I started to think about things. And I thought, 'What a marvellous experience that was!' And I remember I started saying to myself the poem about Abou Ben Adhem: 'Abou Ben Adhem, may his tribe increase, Awoke one night from a deep dream of peace.' That was what I had—a deep dream of peace.[15]

In these modern western examples, as in more ancient and cross-cultural accounts, the guide may act in many roles—as psychopomp (conductor of souls), then as interpreter of the sights that confront the soul upon arrival in the other world. He or she may be something of a teacher and may even take on the role of tour guide—directing the soul from one place to another. For instance, Sogyal Rinpoche in his book, *The Tibetan Book of Living and Dying*, wrote of the phenomenon of the *délok*.

In Tibetan *délok* means 'returned from death', and traditionally *déloks* are people who seemingly 'die' as a result of an illness, and find themselves travelling in the *bardo*. They visit the hell realms, where they witness the judgement of the dead and the sufferings of hell, and sometimes they go to paradises and buddha realms.

They can be accompanied by a deity, who protects them and explains what is happening. After a week the *délok* is sent back to the body with a message from the Lord of Death for the living, urging them to spiritual practice and a beneficial way of life. Often the *déloks* have great difficulty making people believe their story, and they spend the rest of their lives recounting their experiences to others in order to draw them toward the path of wisdom. The biographies of some of the more famous *déloks* were written down, and are sung all over Tibet by travelling minstrels.[16]

Medieval narratives, as we shall see, follow a similar pattern. The guide, in addition to his usual roles, is often called upon to act as protector and deliverer since the medieval other world journey typically passes not only through a heavenly realm as we have seen above in modern western examples, but, as in the Tibetan case, also through the dark domain of hell.[17]

In the eighth century, the vision of Drythelm was recorded by the Anglo-Saxon monk, Bede. Drythelm was a Northumbrian gentleman who, after a severe illness, died one night but, much to the amazement of those gathered around his body, revived at daybreak the next day. They all took fright and ran away; only his wife, who loved him dearly, remained. He reassured her:

Do not be frightened; for I have truly risen from the grasp of death, and I am allowed to live among men again. But henceforth I must not live as I used to, and must adopt a very different way of life.[18]

Drythelm indeed thereafter abandoned the world he had previously known, and entered upon a life of privation and devotion in a Benedictine monastery. But what was the cause of such a dramatic change of heart?

As Drythelm's tale unfolded, his wife heard how he had been escorted by a 'handsome man in a shining robe' to a long, wide, deep valley which he at first mistook for hell. There he saw many suffering souls being tossed backwards and forwards from fierce flames on one side to driving hail and snow on the other. However his guide explained that this was not in fact hell but an intermediate territory, a place of temporary torment for repentant sinners, who could still be saved from further persecution by the intercession of the living on their behalf through masses, prayers and fasts.[19]

Drythelm was then led away from this frightening transitional realm but soon entered an area of intense darkness within which he was only able to find his way by following the radiant presence of his guide. Upon arriving at the gates of hell he saw before him a bottomless pit filled with fire, and as he watched, the souls of the damned were tossed around on the flames like sparks—thrown high up into the air, then plunged straight back down into the putrid depths. As he watched, demonic figures dragged unhappy souls, one after another, into the abyss, and when these malevolent spirits turned towards *him*, he was saved only by the timely reappearance of his guide in the form of a bright star, who frightened them off.

From there Drythelm was led into a more pleasant realm, a world of light, where he found himself in a beautiful meadow. As he approached heaven he could hear angelic singing and:

such was the light flooding all this place that it seemed greater than the brightness of daylight or of the sun's rays at noon.

His guide then told him:

You must now return to your body and live among men once more; but, if you will weigh your actions with greater care and study to keep your words and ways virtuous and simple, then when you die, you too will win a home among these happy spirits that you see.[20]

Of course, testimonials such as this were told and retold to the populace by clerical writers and the church fathers who used them for their own didactic purposes. They were quick to see that stories such as The Vision of Drythelm would make a sure and convincing argument for the need to repent of evil and to embrace the teachings of the church. As Zaleski commented, whatever Drythelm's contribution might have been to the original narrative, Bede's *retelling* of Drythelm's vision can certainly be read as a powerful 'manifesto for Benedictine monasticism, ascetic discipline, and intercessory masses for the dead'.[21] And there are many more stories in the same vein that have similarly been translated into religious instruction.

A prime example is the twelfth century tale about Tundal, a man of staggering sinfulness—even known to be a robber of churches—who, it was believed by all, was inevitably destined for hell. When led into this infernal world of darkness by his angelic guide, Tundal was deserted more than once in order to give him a direct experience of its vile torments and terrors. On one occasion, reminiscent of Drythelm's experience, just as demons were leading him away, he was rescued by the intervention of his guide who appeared as a 'spirit of light' and let it be known that henceforth Tundal would be treated with mercy rather than with the punishment he deserved.

Later he was led into the highest heavenly realms but since he did not yet merit a place in heaven he was told he had to return to his body. His angelic guide then sent him back with the admonishment to remember what he had seen, and to renounce his former way of life.[22]

Another example concerns a man called Stephen, who, dangling from a 'test bridge' over a river of stinking slime, found himself to be the centre of a struggle between good and evil. In view of our recent tour of purgatory and hell in the company of Drythelm and Tundal, I should perhaps digress for a moment to have a closer look at the eternal battle between these two opposing forces.

## Good versus evil

Throughout the ages the opposing forces of good and evil have been vigorously and imaginatively portrayed in the arts. In the western tradition, good is typically represented by Archangel Michael, unsheathed sword in hand, backed up by a luminous legion of angels. In paintings Michael is often portrayed triumphant—with his foot upon a dragon's prostrate body, his lance passing through its maleficent, leathery head.

Evil is typically represented by this same sinewy form—

a fire-breathing dragon with bat-like wings and serpentine tail. And most often this prince of darkness is portrayed surrounded by the maniacal activities of his minions— demonic creatures very much at home amid the pandemonium of hell—chasing, dragging, torturing and tormenting the unhappy souls of sinners.

The medieval 'test bridge' as the name would imply was the locus of a test to differentiate between just and unjust souls. The good were easily identified since they were able to cross the bridge without mishap—Tundal was said to observe a pilgrim priest who made his way to the other side with ease—but sinners were not so fortunate. They would inevitably lose balance, slip, and fall into a slimy mess or fire; or be dragged down by demons into the mouths of fire-breathing beasts waiting below. Some sinners were even physically burdened with articles representative of their wrongdoings, which made their crossing even more difficult. For instance, the wicked Tundal, while attempting to cross a bridge 'two miles long and one palm wide' set with iron spikes, was encumbered with the cow he had stolen from his godfather.[23]

And Stephen, who was observed as he made his way across the bridge, had his foot slip. And as the lower half of his body dangled from the bridge, hideous creatures were seen to come up from below and drag at him in an effort to pull him down. At the same time a company of luminous beings attempted to pull him up by the arms. Apparently the witness of this struggle was at that point sent back to his body so the outcome is unknown. However it is posited that the two sides of Stephen's character were being played out in this drama. His love of almsgiving was being rewarded by the efforts on his behalf by the angelic figures but at the same time his indulgence in all manner of carnal vices was earning him a place in the slime.[24]

The notion that both good and evil angels reside within each of us is widely held. According to Margolies, angels are metaphors for all kinds of human qualities and failings such as love, hate, generosity, greed, lust, hope and fear. He maintains that 'the gathering of angels' set in heaven by John Milton is, according to Jewish teachings, to be found right here on earth within each one of us.[25]

The same idea may also be found in another cultural manifestation. In Zoroastrianism 'good' is represented in the form of the *amesha spentas* or archangels who are named after the many admirable qualities of the Zoroastrian divine being, *Ahura Mazda*. These include *Vohu Manah* (Good Thought or Good Sense), *Armaiti* (Piety or Harmony), and *Asha* (Righteousness or Truth). But since Zoroaster taught that the world is polarised into good and evil, within this world view there is also an opposing force led by the evil *Angra Mainyu* who is represented by entities such as *Druj* (the Lie), whose role is to act specifically in direct opposition to *Asha*.[26]

Swedenborg maintains that the presence of both good and evil forces within us keeps us in balance and provides us with the freedom to choose which direction we want to go in. However he does acknowledge that there is a difference in the way these two entities act. The angels, unlike the demons, do not try to influence us against our will, although they are more than willing to swoop in to protect and defend us, if called upon. By contrast, the demons are said to make every effort to make us suffer, and to enslave and control our every impulse. But as Elisabeth Kübler-Ross says, 'Suffering is like the Grand

Canyon.' If the Grand Canyon had not been carved out by wind and storms throughout the ages it would not be the magnificent monument it is today.

It is so important to understand the role that negative experiences have to play in shaping who we are and who we become in life. Kübler-Ross says:

> If you don't suffer you don't grow. You must
> experience sorrow, loss, tears and anger. Every time you
> go through those, you grow, you progress.
>   One of my guides told me that if he were
> reincarnated, it would be as an infant dying of hunger.
> And I asked him why he wanted to do such a stupid
> thing. He replied that it was to enlarge his sense of
> compassion.[27]

In life we will inevitably find ourselves called upon by both the emissaries of light and the agents of darkness to serve their cause. Carrying love in our hearts seems to be the best defence since the light force of love draws the angels to us and at the same time repels the marauding spirits of darkness. Our challenge, I believe, is to embrace and learn from the periods of darkness sent to help us grow, yet, even while immersed in darkness, to face *always* towards the light.

## Angels as protectors or guardians

In 1992 I went to Japan to confer with researchers about my work on NDEs but while I was there I became interested in the Japanese response to death, in particular to the death of a child. It was in that context that I came across the powerful guardian figure of *Jizo*.

Shortly after my arrival in Tokyo, in a visit to a local temple and burial ground in Azabu-juban, I encountered my first *Jizo*. Although quite ignorant of the significance of this beautiful stone statue with little mounds of pebbles arranged at its feet, it still made a strong impression on me. Soon, however, through seeking out accounts of Japanese childhood NDEs, it became obvious who the statue represented and I began to get a picture of the central role played by *Jizo* within Japanese after-death beliefs.

In all the childhood near-death experiences I located, I found that the child went to the bank of a river, the *sanzu no kawa*, sometimes observed a bridge but was always somehow prevented from crossing to the other side. In one case, a child of high school age had been in a coma for three days. During his near-death experience he found himself on the bank of a river near a very broad, long wooden bridge. As he began to cross the bridge he heard a rhythmic noise approaching from the other side. He then saw a rickshaw man who came up to him, stopped and beckoned him over. But when the boy saw the man's big, fierce face, he took fright, screamed out 'No!' and ran back the way he had come.

This sort of near-death experience is entirely consistent with the Japanese belief that children are not able to cross to the heavenly realms directly. It is believed that they must first spend time in the *Sai-no-Kawara* or 'Dry Bed of the River of Souls', a purgatorial realm where they must do penance. Western parents shudder at the thought but the need for this penance has deep roots in Japanese culture.

The primary relationship in the Japanese family is that

of the mother and child, even beyond death they are still linked by bonds of duty. It is believed that if children die young they must apologise to their mothers for not being able to fulfil their filial duty. And just as the life of a child is overwhelmingly the mother's responsibility, so is that child's death and its spiritual wellbeing in the other world.

It is believed that children cannot cross the *sanzu no kawa* because they are not fully responsible for their own karma until late adolescence. Until then, if they die, they must first do penance until it is time for them to cross. In the otherworld the child's penance consists of piling up stones; while in this world the mother's task is to attend to the spirit of her dead child in a manner reminiscent of the intercessory rites described by Bede.

Mothers go as supplicants to *Jizo* on behalf of their dead children, making offerings, performing ritual practices and saying prayers. Even complete strangers will help by lighting incense and, alongside fresh flowers and other small offerings, placing stones on the little piles at *Jizo*'s feet, in the hope of helping another young soul across the river.

Meanwhile in the Dry Bed of the River of Souls, as fast as the children build their mounds of stones, they are cruelly knocked to the ground by the brutish action of demons. *Jizo*, however, is always there watching over and protecting the children and driving the demons away.

*Jizo* is the bodhisattva[28] of compassion. The Indian equivalent is *Kshitigarbha* whose name literally means 'womb of the earth'. In China, Kshitigarbha is known as *Ti-t'sang*. *Jizo* is also the bodhisattva venerated for saving people from the torments of hell. In fact, near Kamakura there is a famous black *Jizo* who is said to have become blackened by entering the blazing fires of hell to take the place of those who had called for his assistance.

But *Jizo* is best known as the guardian of the souls of deceased children. He is usually represented with a very gentle, compassionate expression on his face. He stands holding in one hand a staff topped by six rings and in the other hand he carries a jewel, sometimes known as a wish-fulfilling stone. In *Myths and Legends of Japan*, F. H. Davis writes:

> Under the earth there is the *Sai-no-Kawara*, or 'the Dry Bed of the River of Souls'. This is the place where all children go after death ... Here the little ones play with the smiling *Jizo*, and here it is that they build small towers of stones ... The mothers of these children, in the world above them, also pile up stones around the images of *Jizo*, for these little towers represent prayers; they are charms against the *oni*, or wicked spirits. Sometimes in the Dry Bed of the River of Souls the *oni* for a moment gain a temporary victory, and knock down the little towers which the ghosts of children have built with so much laughter. When such a misfortune takes place the laughter ceases, and the little ones fly to *Jizo* for protection. He hides them in his long sleeves, and with his sacred staff drives away the red-eyed *oni*.[29]

In Islam the *hafaza* or guardian angels play a similar role, also protecting people from the troublesome activities of the *jinn* or demons. However in this case it is believed that in life everyone has four *hafaza* assigned to them—two to watch over them during the day and two at night.

It is said however, that at dusk and dawn people are least protected since, during the changing of the guard, the *jinn* are always on the lookout for a moment of inattention in order to create havoc in people's lives.[30]

Belief in the existence of guardian angels is of long standing and is very widespread. Zoroastrians had protective spirits called *fravashis* and pre-Christian Romans believed that everyone had a guardian spirit—every woman protected by a *juno* and every man by a *genius*. Greeks believed that at birth everyone was assigned a *daemon* who looked after and guided them throughout life. And in shamanic cultures the guardian, protective, tutelary spirit typically took (and still takes) the form of an animal, bird or reptile. Thomas Aquinas taught that individuals are always accompanied by a guardian angel and since beginning this project I have had many Catholics tell me that the notion of guardian angels was very much a part of their childhood religious instruction.[31]

Angela, the teenager who suffered a fractured skull when she was hit by a hockey ball, maintains that she has always been aware of being protected.

> Ever since I was young I've always felt that I've had protectors. I was scared of dying, and other things, I guess, but for some reason I've always had a peace about me because I've always felt as though there've been people protecting me.
>
> When I was in hospital I actually felt that there were people in the room with me. There wasn't anyone there but I could feel a real presence of somebody there looking after me.
>
> My brother and I are extremely close. He's in the

army and he got compassionate leave to come home to
see me. I'd been completely out of it for days. Then
this day I felt something at the end of my bed saying,
'Angela, wake up!' I felt there was somebody waking
me up. It felt like a big kick at the end of my bed, like
somebody just moved and shook my bed. I opened my
eyes and looked around the room but there was
nobody there. Then I looked over at the door and my
brother walked in!

I actually hadn't wanted him to come back because I
didn't want him to see me the way I was. But Mum
insisted. And here I was, woken up just before he
arrived.

I've had so many of those experiences especially
while I was in hospital. I *know* there was somebody
there looking after me all the time.

And Bill, a forty-five-year-old salesman, told me:

I always believe someone up there really likes me
because quite often I'm in strife and something or
someone always seems to turn up to help me out.
Sometimes I even feel someone leads me by the hand.

Craig Lundahl records the story of a late nineteenth
century Mormon missionary who, while stricken with
malaria, had a near-death experience during which he saw
his guardian angel. This being told him that he had been
following him constantly while on earth and was there now
to report his presence in the other world.[32] And in a ninth

century tale—the Vision of Wetti—the angelic guide, towards the end of Wetti's otherworld journey, revealed himself to be his guardian angel with the words, 'I am he who was ordered to watch over you'.[33]

'Watching over' is probably the primary role associated with guardian angels and has been depicted, particularly in Victorian times, in familiar scenes of children sheltering under the wing of a luminous angelic figure, but some tell of a more active involvement by their angels. Some angels take part in supernatural rescues.

## Angels as rescuers

In the twelfth chapter of Acts in the *Bible*, we find Peter, imprisoned by King Herod, under heavy guard. The night before he was to be executed, Peter was asleep between two soldiers, while two others were stationed at the door to his cell. Suddenly he was awakened by an angel.

> Suddenly an angel of the Lord appeared and a light shone in the cell. He tapped Peter on the side and woke him, saying, 'Get up quickly.' And the chains fell off his wrists. The angel said to him, 'Fasten your belt and put on your sandals.' He did so. Then he said to him, 'Wrap your cloak around you and follow me.' Peter went out and followed him; he did not realize that what was happening with the angel's help was real; he thought he was seeing a vision.
>
> After they had passed the first and the second guard, they came before the iron gate leading into the city. It opened for them of its own accord, and they went outside and walked along a lane, when suddenly the

angel left him. Then Peter came to himself and said, 'Now I am sure that the Lord has sent his angel and rescued me from the hands of Herod.'

In the *Bible* there are numerous accounts of angels who bring about miraculous rescues. Another is recorded in the third chapter of Daniel. Here we are told that King Nebuchadnezzar had an enormous gold statue set up on the plain of Dura in Babylon. He called upon all his provincial officials to attend its dedication and commanded that they all prostrate themselves before it. And he warned, 'Whoever does not fall down and worship shall immediately be thrown into a furnace of blazing fire.'

It soon came to King Nebuchadnezzar's attention that three men—Shadrach, Meshach and Abednego—had refused to worship the golden idol set up on the plain. The king was furious and ordered that the furnace be 'heated up seven times more than was customary' and that the men be bound and thrown into the fire. The furnace was so hot that the guards who approached it to throw in the three men were themselves instantly killed. But Shadrach, Meshach and Abednego, still fully clad and securely bound were seen to fall into the fire.

King Nebuchadnezzar watched in amazement as all of a sudden a fourth man appeared in the fire. And that fourth man was an angel. He called out to his counsellors:

Was it not three men that we threw bound into the fire?' They answered the king, 'True, O king.' He replied, 'But I see four men unbound, walking in the middle of the fire, and they are not hurt; and the fourth has the appearance of a god.'

Nebuchadnezzar then ordered that the men come out of the furnace and Shadrach, Meshach and Abednego emerged, completely unscathed. It could be seen by all that 'the fire had not had any power over the bodies of those men; the hair of their heads was not singed, their tunics were not harmed, and not even the smell of fire came from them'. Nebuchadnezzar said:

> Blessed be the God of Shadrach, Meshach and
> Abednego, who has sent his angel and delivered his
> servants who trusted in him.

This story reminds me of a supernatural rescue I read over ten years ago in Raymond Moody's book, *Reflections on Life after Life*. The account was related to Moody by a man who, in a terrible industrial accident, had been trapped in a huge vat. At the time the vat was being filled by a stream of acid and steam which was being pumped in at high pressure. He recalled:

> The heat of all this was terrific ... I had gotten as far as
> I could into a corner but the stuff was so hot that it
> was burning me through my clothing. So, at that time I
> realized that in just a matter of minutes I would be
> scalded to death.
>     I guess it was in my weakness or whatever that I
> gave up. To myself, I just said, 'This is it. I'm a goner.'
> I could not see, and the heat was so intense that I could
> not open my eyes. I had my eyes closed the whole
> time. But it seemed that the whole area lit up with a
> glow. And a verse of Scripture that I had heard all my

life, that had never meant too much to me, 'Lo, I am with thee always,' came from a direction which later turned out to be the only way out.

I couldn't stand to open my eyes, but I could still see that light, so I followed it. I know that my eyes were closed the whole time, though. The doctor didn't even treat my eyes later. No acid got in them.

After I got back to work, some of the people who work there were talking about how calm I was after the whole thing had happened. I'm not that brave a man; I don't have that much courage. The fact that I was led by an unseen hand out of the danger was the source of my courage, was the calmness they saw ... [I know] that it was God's will that my life be spared, for what reason, I don't know. At that time I was not living as close to God as I should have. I have been drawn closer to him by this.[34]

Except that it happened in this world, the situation described above could well take its place among the more usual tortures and torments we find in medieval tales of terrifying otherworldly experiences. For instance, it would sit easily alongside the hellish experiences outlined in the sixth century by Gregory the Great, even down to the desire to live life differently afterwards. In one of Gregory's most famous anecdotes, he tells of a hermit who had a close call in hell. Just as this man was being dragged into the flames to join several others already dangling in the fire, 'an angel in a shining garment' swooped in to save him. And in a manner typical of the medieval narratives we have already seen, the angel then left him with the usual suggestion that he should be careful, from now on, how he lived his life.[35]

William Serdahely records the story of Eric, who as a five-year-old child, fell into the water between a barge and a tugboat. Unable to swim, he was calmed by a reassuring voice and the presence of a vertical 'shaft' of white light that covered his body and seemed to be there for him to climb. The voice said, 'Climb the stairs, climb the stairs.' And when he did as he was told he emerged at the surface.[36]

In Eric's story the angel manifested as a light and a voice but sometimes angels can swoop to the rescue quite unseen and unheard, yet still nudge us into action. Some years ago I was sitting in a small open-top car in the yard of a sawmill, enjoying the sunshine while waiting for a friend. I was aware that one of the workers was manoeuvring an enormous bulldozer laden with uncut logs but I was just sitting there calmly not paying any particular attention to what he was doing. All of a sudden I found myself leaping out of the car. Within seconds the car was flattened. The bulldozer driver had lost control of his vehicle. I saw nothing and heard nothing but was simply *compelled* to leave the car.

Sophie Burnham tells a similar story of a man who had been sitting in his car after it had broken down on a major highway, waiting for a tow truck. Suddenly he felt an incredible urge to leave the car, to get some coffee at a nearby diner. He had gone no more than a few steps when a truck came out of nowhere and smashed the car to pieces.[37]

Journalist, Pierre Jovanovic, writes in his book, *An Inquiry into the Existence of Guardian Angels*, that many of his journalistic colleagues—especially war correspondents and photographers—had also experienced inexplicable supernatural rescues. Jovanovic had just such an experience in August 1988 when he was travelling along a highway in Silicon Valley. His female companion was driving and he was in the front passenger seat when suddenly, without thinking, he flung himself to the left. A second later a sniper's bullet pierced the windscreen, right where he'd been sitting.[38] In a similarly surprising escape, a reporter in Beirut in 1976, was sitting at a barricade talking with a Palestinian soldier. The soldier was also seated, with his Kalashnikov rifle resting across his knees, the barrel at about the level of the reporter's legs. They were both sitting there, chatting and drinking coffee, when 'on a sudden impulse' the reporter leapt to his feet. At that instant the Kalashnikov went off. They couldn't work out why it happened but if the reporter had not jumped up there is no doubt he would have been seriously wounded.[39]

One young woman, Taylor, wrote to me of the many angel experiences she had had throughout her life.

I was an abused child and often spent time alone. At times I was psychic. And I could feel the angels in the room with me whenever I needed comfort.

I am twenty-one years old now and I have three children—a girl (five years old), a boy (three years old) and another boy (two years old).

At the time of this angel experience I was seven months pregnant with my third child and my daughter was in hospital with pneumonia. I'd promised to spend the night with her. I was feeling very uneasy all day. Three people had offered to take me to the hospital but then all of a sudden nobody could drive me there. So I decided to walk the hour it took to walk there.

When I came to the main road, if I went one way I'd be home in five minutes—I'd started walking from my mother-in-law's place—or if I went the other way I'd be at the hospital in half an hour. I started to feel really scared and then something pushed me and said, 'Go home!' very loudly and demandingly. Twice it said this. But I just couldn't break my promise to my little girl when she was so sick, so I continued on.

Soon I came to a zebra crossing. I waited for the cars to stop then I walked in front of the first car. I had only taken a couple of steps in front of the second car when it was hit from behind by another car doing sixty kilometres an hour. In the panic he'd put his foot on the accelerator before the brakes.

At that instant I knew it was on or under the car for me so I threw myself onto the bonnet. At first I screamed then I was just quiet. Those few seconds lasted an eternity for me. I thought about so much. There wasn't a person or place I didn't think about. Most people describe this as 'my life flashed before my eyes' but it's just so much more than that.

Then I heard a voice and it said, 'Yes or no?' And I just knew it meant, 'Yes, I want to live or no I don't want to live'. And I said, 'Yes.' I actually spoke the word but not through my mouth and not in my mind, perhaps with my spirit. I don't know, but I did say 'yes'.

Then I realised that time was slowly coming back to normal and I was falling head-first off the bonnet and I was staring directly at a headlight. Then I felt my head being held as I was 'placed' beside the car. It was just so gentle.

Apparently I rode for thirty or forty feet on the bonnet of the car and the police accident investigation people said they can't understand how I'm alive. They think that I should have been dead or severely injured, but I only had some scratches, bruises and a weak knee. My son was born healthy four weeks later.

This experience has helped me to always listen to the 'invisible voice'. I was warned and ignored it and as a result my unborn son and I could both have died but we were lucky that day because God sent his angels down to help us.

A friend sent me an article from a New Zealand newspaper relating a very similar story. Apparently a young mother who was three months pregnant at the time was celebrating Christmas day with a large group of family members. They were all standing outside on the second floor deck of the family home when the deck suddenly collapsed and everyone fell to the ground. Five people were injured, two of them seriously, but the young woman, who sustained a severely bruised pelvis and a swollen ankle, said an angel had cushioned her landing and comforted her as she lay injured. Her baby also survived. She said the angel was a tall man dressed in white but she couldn't see his face or if he had wings.[40]

In yet another example, an eight-year-old girl, Marilyn, who had been hit by a car, was tossed into the air, hit the ground and then rolled over and over and over until, much to everyone's amazement, she came to rest right at the edge of an open sewer. The parents, who were watching horrified as these events unfolded, could not understand how she could possibly have avoided falling *into* the sewer since she was going at such a speed as she rolled towards it.

Later as they were telling all of this to the doctor, the

child said, 'But didn't you see that huge, beautiful angel standing in the sewer, holding up her hands to keep me from rolling in?'[41]

In 1988 I interviewed a doctor who had survived a near-death episode. At the time she also described an angelic rescue she and a friend had experienced one day as they were driving to a conference.

My friend, James, and I were driving down the highway on our way to a conference. About halfway we changed drivers and while James was driving, a very drunk guy hit us at more than a hundred miles an hour. We were doing probably eighty at the time, on the expressway. James didn't panic. He was actually very level-headed and just tried to steer us out of the collision.

Even though the car that bumped us was going in the same direction, it managed to bump into us three times. And all the while James was trying to get us off onto the shoulder of the road. Finally we hit a post.

After it was all over we were just sitting there. Both of us were giggly, like little kids on bubbly water. We felt sure that there'd been something slowing the car down, sort of like a big creature with wings, beating a wind at the car. We felt it. And we also saw a light, sort of a bit like sunlight, streaming through the woods, through the trees. It was an extraordinary feeling. It was very close. I tell you, it brings goosebumps up to remember it. The guy in the other car didn't even stop!

I didn't sleep for days. Both of us had the powerful impression that there was a being with wings, maybe more than one, braking the velocity of the car. And we were both unscathed apart from terrible bruises where the seatbelts held us. If we'd been thrown out of the car we wouldn't have stood a chance.

## Angels as healers

Raphael is the angel most often associated with healing. In I Enoch 40:9, Enoch has a vision of the four great archangels, one of whom is Raphael, and is told that Raphael is 'set over all the diseases and all the wounds of humankind'. But Raphael is not only the healer of human bodies, he is also the healer of their spirits; and of any other problems they have in their lives.

In the Apocryphal Book of Tobit we see Raphael in action. This book tells the story of Tobit, a pious blind man, who wanted his son, Tobias, to go on a mission to recover some money held in trust for him in Media. Since Tobias was not familiar with the way, he went out to find a travelling companion and hired the angel, Raphael, (who was waiting at his door) believing him to be a kinsman. When Tobit heard of this man, he wanted to meet him, and so Tobias brought Raphael before his father. During their conversation, Tobit bemoaned his blindness and Raphael somewhat mysteriously told him: 'Take courage; the time is near for God to heal you.'(5:10)

After taking their leave, Tobias and the angel, Raphael, accompanied by a small dog, headed off on their journey. The first night they camped by a river, and while there, a big fish jumped out and tried to bite Tobias on the foot. Raphael called out for him to keep hold of the fish. 'So the young man grasped the fish and drew it up on the land.' (6:4) Raphael then proceeded to have him cut it open and remove its gall, heart and liver, which he said were all useful as medicine.

They then continued on their way. At one point Tobias asked Raphael to explain the medicinal value of the fish organs. How could they be used to heal? Raphael replied:

> As for the fish's heart and liver, you must burn them to
> make a smoke in the presence of a man or woman
> afflicted by a demon or evil spirit, and every affliction
> will flee away and never remain with that person any
> longer. And as for the gall, anoint a person's eyes
> where white films have appeared on them; blow upon
> them, upon the white films, and the eyes will be healed.
> (6:8-9)

The first remedy was to be used by Tobias much sooner than expected, since not long after this exchange Raphael informed him they would shortly arrive at the home of a kinsman whose daughter Sarah, he was to marry. Understandably Tobias was not keen to marry Sarah since it was well known that she had already had seven husbands, all of whom died on the wedding night. Raphael reassured him that he would be in no danger from evil spirits if he burned the fish heart and liver on the embers of the incense and prayed to God. The odour would drive away the demons and the marriage bed would be safe. It all came to pass as Raphael said and there was healing and rejoicing on their wedding night. (8:1-18)

The next day Raphael left Tobias with Sarah, and travelled on alone to collect Tobit's money. Then, after rejoining them for fourteen days of marriage celebrations, they all set off together on the return journey. As they approached the home of Tobit, Raphael stopped for a moment and instructed Tobias in the use of the fish gall so that he could heal his father's blindness. He said:

> I know that his eyes will be opened. Smear the gall of the fish on his eyes; the medicine will make the white films shrink and peel off from his eyes, and your father will regain his sight and see the light. (11:8)

Once again it all came to pass as Raphael had said and there was healing and rejoicing in Tobit's household. It was only then that Raphael revealed to the two men his true identity as an emissary from God.

> I will now declare the whole truth to you and will conceal nothing from you ... When you and Sarah prayed it was I who brought and read the record of your prayer before the glory of the Lord ... I was sent to you to test you. And at the same time God sent me to heal you and Sarah, your daughter-in-law. I am Raphael, one of the seven angels who stand ready and enter before the glory of the Lord.
>    The two of them were shaken; they fell face down for they were afraid. But he said to them, 'Do not be afraid; peace be with you.' (12:11-18)

Recently I came across the story of Ann, a cancer sufferer, who had a mysterious visitor arrive at her door in much the same way as Raphael had arrived in Tobit's life. This stranger, a black man with blue eyes, addressed her by name, saying that he'd been sent by God to tell her that her cancer had been healed. He said that his name was Thomas and that before he left he would pray for her. Thomas then stretched his hand out towards her and as he did this, the heat and power emanating from his hand was so strong that she felt herself falling to the floor. As she lay there she could feel a cleansing light pass through every part of her body. Then the man disappeared. Ann immediately reached for the phone to contact her doctor, and not long after, she was told her cancer had vanished.[42]

And some years ago, while I was still editing the newsletter for a support group of near-death experiencers, I received the following account of an angelic healing from Fiona. She wrote:

I was fifteen years old when I was admitted to hospital after a long illness, I had glandular fever, hepatitis and tonsilitis. The tonsilitis was so bad that the doctor said it was the closest he'd seen to diphtheria in years.

As my throat had closed over to the point where I was having difficulty getting liquid down, the doctor was trying to decide whether to do a tracheotomy then and there or wait till morning. He decided to wait, unless I got worse through the night. He then left and the nurse settled me down for the night. As it was really quite late, my Mum went home and I went to sleep.

I was woken some time later by a light shining over me. My first thought was that the nurse must have left the light over the bed on but when I looked, it was very definitely off. I can't describe where this glow was coming from, I was bathed from head to toe in this wondrous and beautiful glow. It was just there, completely covering me, engulfing me in its warmth and beauty. It was just incredible . . . truly breathtaking.

I then realised I was not alone. To my right, standing next to the head of the bed was a presence, I dubbed it my guardian angel. This presence gave me a feeling of such love and security! It was so very special, and I felt special. I just felt a complete and total love that's hard to describe. I then straightaway fell into a peaceful sleep and awoke the next morning refreshed.

When the doctor arrived bright and early the next morning to check my throat he had a look and was astounded at what he saw—my throat had cleared up completely. He looked again and then asked the nurse to have a look. She said, 'Yes doctor, it's clear.'

I never told anyone what happened to me that night, certainly not the doctor. And, as amazing as [that experience] was, I never really dwelt on it, I simply accepted it.

Some healings such as Tobit's and Ann's and Fiona's occur when an angel comes to *this* world but some people are healed during a visit to the world of angels. Olivia, who was suffering from meningitis at the time, described to me an experience of healing she had which took place in the world of light.

This particular night I had a meditation group meeting. I was going to call it off because I was feeling extremely ill, but I didn't. Several people commented on the fact that I wasn't looking well. This was a group of people who were developing. I am a trance medium but at that stage I was withholding going into deep trance because I was helping the others. There was a group of maybe ten or twelve people in the room and as we went into meditation I was aware that I was going in very deeply. It was a pulling feeling, a feeling of being pulled up, through something. And I thought, 'I can't do this in the group.' But it didn't make any difference, I still went. I was being pulled up through a tunnel, and there was a light at the top, glowing, and I went through into it. (Just before I went into that tunnel, or into the light, I remember thinking, 'I'm not breathing.' But then I went and I had no control over it.)

I was surrounded by the light that time, and, it sounds poetic but it's exactly as I saw it, there was a circle of hands coming through the light. I was in the middle of them and they were all held out towards me. They were individual hands and the palms were up very gently and they were all glowing. It was the most incredible feeling, it really was. I still can't talk about it even now without getting emotional because there was an enormous amount of love there. It was pure love and pure light. That's the only way I can describe it.

I was in the middle and the hands were all held out towards me. There was nothing spoken, yet there was a communication in my mind. I didn't hear the words in a voice ... but the words were there in my mind. I asked if I was dying and the answer I got back was, 'No, it isn't time yet.' I was told that this would be a turning point and from here on I would recover, I'd get better. I asked if I could stay there because it was beautiful, it was just so beautiful, but the answer was that it wasn't time, that I had to go back. So I came back. I think I must have received a lot of healing that night, because after that experience I did start to get better.

Healing is always available from the angels. All we have to do is ask. This does not mean that the healing will be instantaneous, or even that it will take the form we expect. It may seem in each of the three cases above that the healing *was* instantaneous, that it *did* happen out of the blue but we must remember that we do not know the full story— we are not privy to the inner life of the person concerned. We do not know what preceded or followed that healing. Indeed, sometimes death, the ultimate healing, may be an inevitable part of the process. But whatever the long-term outcome is meant to be, the point I want to make here is that wholehearted participation in the 'healing journey' is far more important than dogged attachment to the singular goal of 'being healed' in the traditional sense.

It is too often forgotten that illness occurs on more than the physical level. It always has physical, mental and spiritual components, which all need to be addressed for a true healing to take place. So in addition to seeking the advice of traditional medicine, we also need to take responsibility for ourselves and be prepared to do our own *inner* work. But we are not alone on our journey—the angels are always there for us, ready to help heal not just our bodies but also our lives.

In my experience the healing journey can be incredibly important for spiritual growth since a period of unwellness, confusion and despair will often herald a spiritual opening and movement to a higher level of consciousness. I've seen this played out in the lives of so many—in the lives of grieving parents and their afflicted children, dying people in hospices, cancer sufferers and even otherwise healthy people suddenly struck down with the 'flu or, more seriously, with a mysterious disorder such as chronic fatigue syndrome. Whatever the illness, when we are unwell we need to take it as a signal to rest and examine our lives. I don't suggest this in a blaming way—it's very easy to blame the victim or even blame ourselves for getting sick—but I do feel strongly that, whatever the cause of the illness, it is always an opportunity for growth. After all, ill health at whatever level inevitably stops us in our tracks, stops the never-ending flow of daily chatter and provides the angels with an opportunity to get through to us, so the least we can do is listen to what they have to say.

In 1996 my own state of health was very fragile. I had just finished writing *Beloved Visitors* and it is obvious to me, now, that I was suffering 'burnout'. In addition to the effort of writing the book and the four years of working with grieving parents, a very dear friend of mine passed away the following week. That same week I had an overseas guest arriving and I had to travel to another state to fulfill some speaking engagements. I felt awash with grief and totally exhausted. Very quickly this exhaustion took on the form of a bad back and two frozen shoulders. The pain was terrible and I was very soon immobilised, unable to do many of life's most basic tasks. The message was loud and clear. Be still! It took a while to sink in but once I had accepted the situation, I declared myself willing to learn whatever I needed to learn, and to do whatever was needed.

Even at the beginning I knew I was being forced to take time out for a reason: I was being prepared for the next stage of my life and work. Past experience had taught me that much! And, if ever I had any doubts, I was reminded of this constantly in my shamanic guidance, both from my power animal and, increasingly, from the angels. However, from time to time, I became impatient to start working again but I was told again and again to be still, to relinquish control and to trust. Trust was apparently a big issue.

In July that year I was told by the angels that one major contributing factor to my state of ill-health was lack of trust. It took some time for me to understand in what sense 'trust' was being used. At first I understood it to mean that I should *trust* that all that was happening was right for me. And at a deep level I did know that. But several months later, once I began seeing a Feldenkrais practitioner and practising the lessons at home, I saw clearly how full of fear my body had become. The freezing of my shoulders and back was in response to fear. I hardly dared move in case I crumpled under the burden I was carrying. I felt unsupported. I felt that if I didn't 'hold myself up', 'support myself', et cetera, that I would 'break' or 'fall apart'. From the moment of that realisation I knew it was safe to move again, to let go of my fears and let the next stage begin. Of course that was only the beginning, and recovery was a long, slow journey.

I opened myself totally to the process. In addition to my daily practice of Feldenkrais lessons, I continued doing Yoga nidra, and meditating for two, three or four hours a day. During meditation I regularly got flashes of angel faces and wings and I would also receive messages that were encouraging or enlightening, or both. One day I was told

to open Gitta Mallasz's *Talking with Angels* and the message
was:

> But if body and Light, the human and the Divine, are
> *united*, the wound is no longer needed, for then the
> Blood circulates and Heaven and earth are joined.
> Until this occurs, the wound pains. But union is now
> possible!
> Behold, the wound is no longer needed! May the
> wound be healed![43]

During my shamanic journeys I was almost always met
by angels, who would stroke my shoulders before taking
me to the Upperworld. On one occasion, upon arrival in
the Upperworld, my teacher was waiting for me. He smiled
gently, then placed one hand on each of my shoulders and,
as he did this, I could feel the melting warmth of light
pouring into them. He then put his hands on the back of
my neck and poured love in there. And then I was told,
'Be true, be steadfast and stay always in the light'. I
wondered 'true' to what? And the answer was 'true to your
path'. A message I was to receive again and again.

Over a period of twelve months I frequently saw Chamuel
(the Angel of Divine Love) in the Upperworld during my
shamanic journeys and also in meditation. Occasionally I
would just see the colour pink but usually I would see
Chamuel in his full angelic glory standing before me. On
one occasion I had cause to ask Chamuel for some urgent
advice and healing. I hesitate to mention this episode because
I don't like to give energy to the dark forces but they do
exist and we need to be aware of their strength. And we

also need to be aware that the healing love of angels is stronger.

I was visiting another city at the time and had been interviewing a person who had told me he was well acquainted with angels. But as we talked, I could feel he was filled with darkness and was attempting to bring all the forces of darkness to bear on me, trying to draw me into his world. I resisted but by the time the interview was over I felt quite shaken by the experience and I was left with a fluttering, breathless feeling in my heart chakra. Straightaway I returned to my hotel room and did a shamanic journey to ask for healing.

When I arrived in the Upperworld, Chamuel was there to meet me. Immediately he wrapped his arms and wings around me until I could feel the warmth of his light suffusing every cell in my body. Next he removed a sword from my heart. A sword! He filled the wound with pink healing light surrounded me with pink healing light and cleansed my aura. He then told me to bathe myself, wash my hair, destroy the interview tape, my notes and anything to do with this person.

When I returned to the normal state of consciousness I immediately did as I had been instructed and miraculously felt quite restored, completely cleansed and free of this man's influence.

Interestingly, the night before, I had given a public talk and afterwards several people had approached me to say they had seen a huge angel, about ten feet tall, with blue wings standing directly behind me the whole time I was speaking. Another person saw brilliant blue eyes shining through my eyes. Since Archangel Michael is associated with the colour blue and is often known as the warrior whose light triumphs over darkness, I couldn't help wondering if he had been there to protect me from this man who was sitting in the audience directly in front of me.

On the same trip, in another city, I went to see a Feldenkrais practitioner. As the treatment proceeded I became conscious that Chamuel was present in the room and was overseeing the work this woman was doing. At one point she said she could see colour all around me—in her words, the colour of heart. I asked her later what she had seen and she said she saw me completely swathed in pink. I then told her of Chamuel's presence and of the pink light that he leaves in his wake. She was quite excited by this and said she felt the way she'd worked with me that day was showing her that she could always work like that. She saw her future before her and it was full of joy. So, as Chamuel was healing me, he was also filling another life with his blessings.

A few days later I returned home and, as was often the case in those days, as soon as I arrived back in the city I began to feel downhearted. But I continued my spiritual practices nonetheless, and the healing continued. In the diary the angels had instructed me to keep I wrote:

Been a strange few days. Feel I've lost my rhythm. Unhappy back in the city. Having trouble sleeping again. Don't enjoy all the people, the noise, the dirty air. Lost my rhythm. Shoulders aching. Going to take a while to get back in the groove.

A week later, though, I did a space clearing ceremony in the apartment and felt the energy begin to sparkle once

again. And that night I did a shamanic journey. Afterwards
I wrote in my diary:

> I received a gentle welcome and then I asked would my
> shoulders be healed soon. The angel lifted my arms out
> at right angles as though I was lifting my wings, then
> forwards above my head and then right back and down.
> In other words 'Yes'. Something like this happened
> once before but this time I had a marvellous sense of
> freedom and movement. It was *so* vivid. Then he took
> me flying. We flew over very green countyside that
> reminded me of the gentle slopes around Eden's place.
> So I asked where I should be living now. As I asked
> the question I realised I'd asked about 'now'. I then
> saw my apartment from outside and high above. It
> radiated light and was sparkling and filled with light.
> I accepted this. Very interesting. A very clear message
> that I should still be here for the time being. This has
> taken away doubts about whether I should be doing
> something about moving.

Soon after, a friend did a shamanic journey for me. She
was told that the symbol of discernment is sage—wisdom
of the heart. She asked why I had this pain and the angel
answered, 'It's because of all the crosses she's been carrying,
other people's crosses. She's had heart but not wisdom of
the heart.' He then began pulling them out. He said I
should be like the desert. I should lay myself open and let
extraneous things fall away and be at one with the Great
Spirit. 'To be a light bearer,' he said, 'you have to be light
and not carry heavy things.' This friend then saw a jug of

something being poured over me. It was a jug of grace and the angels said that I was in a state of grace.

About the same time another stage of my healing began when I was told by the angels that I was to use my hands for healing. I felt a bit silly at first, and very presumptuous, but I began practising on family and friends. I was taught a lot in a very short time and I was constantly amazed by the results. And the feeling of energy coming through. The sense of the presence of angels during those healing sessions was incredibly strong. Occasionally I would even see one supervising me. I was told one day, 'Use your hands for healing two or three times a week being very aware that you are just letting the energies flow through you'. And I was thanked for my trust and willingness to let them work through me. I was thanked for my *trust!* I could hardly believe it. Then I was told that as the healing energies passed through me to others, I was also being healed.

So the healing continued. It was a long and often painful process but during that time my shamanic practice and healing work was transformed. And when I look back and see that my relationship with the angels, this book, my new home and many new friendships, all emerged as a result of this profound inner journey, I feel very blessed.

# 6

# *Living in the Company of Angels*

### *Telling others*

When she was forty-six years old Juliet had a near-death experience during which she heard a noise like wings flapping and then found herself in a magnificent forest in the company of beautiful angelic beings. She had a wonderful sense of homecoming but was told that she had to return to her body—there was a lot more for her to do. She said:

> The next morning, one of the nurses was walking past—she'd just come on duty—she was walking past the door and then she came back and looked in. She came over to me and said, 'What's happened to you?' She said, 'I was walking past and when I looked in I could see this glow around you.'
>
> I told her what'd happened. I didn't know whether

she was going to laugh or not. And she said, 'Yes I believe you, it happens.'

Juliet was fortunate that someone responded so sensitively to her experience but this is not always the case. Seven-year-old Kayla told me that when she tried to tell some friends at school about the angel she had seen, they thought she was 'stupid' and one boy said, 'Oh sure!' And twelve year-old Renée recalled, 'Last year I talked to some kids about my angel and they got spooked. And since then they think I'm weird so . . . it's hard for me to find friends now.' Renée didn't even tell her mother about it for quite a while because she was afraid she'd think she was 'a bit looney'. She said, 'I could see angels and stuff but I never really told Mum about it because I thought she'd get a bit frightened of it. But to me it felt very comforting.'

Even adults can be reticent about telling others of their experiences. Beth said:

> In the flush of the excitement you do tend to talk a bit about it and people put you down or try and tell you logically that it can't be. But I knew I hadn't made it up— it was my experience—so I became a little cautious about who I told. But I reached the stage where if I did tell someone and they didn't believe it, that didn't bother me because I knew it was true. It was my truth and that was that.

Olivia has come to believe quite strongly that these experiences need to be 'brought up front and focussed on and accepted as normal'. She said:

It's not a kooky experience, it doesn't mean you've flipped. It doesn't mean that you're going into nervous breakdown cycles. Unfortunately that's exactly what some people think. But I have no compunction these days in saying to people that I've had angel experiences, and that I hope to have a lot more!

But I understand that it's pretty overwhelming for the average person. Even with the spiritual background I have, something in me fought angels really hard. You see I'm a Capricorn so I'm pretty down-to-earth. That helps at times but it also hinders because I really have to prove these things to myself.

And Lisa said:

If you tell people these days that you speak to your angel, everyone goes, 'Right, here's a nice little padded room for you'. The problem is our supposed sophistication.

The one thing I learned with my experiences is to stop questioning and to start listening. You learn to shut up and listen to what they're saying. I don't think the angels ever stopped talking to us, we just stopped listening.

## After-effects

People who have had an angel encounter are always greatly changed by it. While it is happening they may be overwhelmed and wonder-stricken, they may be emotional or excited, or they may simply be filled with a blissful sense of comfort and peace. But, whatever the content of the experience, afterwards, with both feet planted firmly on the ground again, they inevitably begin to look at their lives afresh.

Jim told me that his angel experiences have always been incredibly gentle.

> They always show me that I'm surrounded by light, a light that comes from above, and they let me know that I am being looked after, that I'm secure. Secure in their love. [Emotional] This is very hard to talk about.

Jim has received messages from angels in several different forms energy, voice and vision, but his visions have always been the strongest and clearest. Apparently as a child Jim had a considerable level of psychic ability but as soon as he entered his teenage years he lost it.

> It came back when I was about twenty-two but, soon after that, I began developing my business approach and got right into making money. I pushed myself too hard and I lost my vision again.
>
> When the angels came to me it's as though there was a tap on my door saying, 'You've got to listen.' You see, by then I was very driven. I was always working, totally involved in business things and getting very little sleep. I thought money was the be-all but then, after the experiences began, I started to see that in terms of my life, all this work and even the money was not doing me any good.
>
> I was trained as a toolmaker, and I've worked around plastics and racing cars, and structural

steelworks, and now I feel my angel guide is teaching me how to make things that will be advantageous to mankind. So far I've been given little pieces of a jigsaw puzzle and I feel I have to work with them until I know how they go together. There are pieces I've made that I haven't finished yet. I'm still waiting for more information. You see, they tend to give me a lesson then wait till I've digested it before they give me the next one.

There's no disputing that these experiences have happened for a purpose. I see my life's work so differently now. If I could open up more and receive the information without ego getting in the way I could use that information for the betterment of man instead of using it only for greed and money. That's where I believe all this is taking me but I need to take time over it, and make sure I process it correctly.


Another man, Michael, also commented on how his work was affected by his experiences with angels. He said:

These experiences have changed my priorities absolutely. They've caused havoc! My job has just about had it because of changed priorities. It used to be everything to me. It used to come first before anything. Absolutely first. But now it's just about last. Now I consider my job just a means to do other things rather than as the thing I do. This makes it a bit difficult financially but I always know that things are going to be okay, I'm always being shown. Once we were totally

short of money and the bills were coming in, then I
won what we needed in a lottery! Crazy things like
that happen all the time.

My experiences have been totally uplifting and
they've moved me absolutely out of the path I was on.
They've shown me that I need to evolve.


Lisa told me that she feels her experiences with Raphael
have put her on a path towards the light.

I've always been a very volatile person but now I'm a
lot calmer, a lot more accepting. I used to be so angry
at the world.

I never scoffed at the spiritual world but I didn't ever
feel I was a part of it. It was always something that
happened to other people, but now I'm one of those
people. The peace and the acceptance of myself is just
the most amazing thing.

In the past it used to be that *things* were important.
Things that I had to have. I never earned a great salary
but I still had to have things. But now what's important
is time with people, time to be able to sit and look at
the water. To see a sunset, a moonrise.

I look back through my old journals and I think,
'Wow that used to be me!' I was so angry! Back then I
would press so hard on the pen I'd go through five or
six pages! Where's that anger now?

When I look at what I write in my journals now, it's
all my observations of nature and peace. Until you walk
away and look back you really can't see what's going
on. What was I so angry about? There wasn't anything

in particular, I was just angry. But I'm no longer there and it's just the most amazing feeling.

And Juliet said that after her experience she was left with 'a wonderful feeling of peace', and 'knowing'.

You don't know what you know but you know something. [laughs] And such a feeling of tranquillity. The feeling that it's okay, everything's okay. It was an overwhelming feeling and it's stayed with me.

Caitlin feels that she's much more aware and more open since her experiences, and a lot more tolerant. And Diana says that she now feels stronger and more at ease in the world. She said:

It's been such a life-changing thing. I think I walked around for at least five or six months with a feeling of total happiness. It was the first time in a long time that I felt totally serene and totally happy. That's a long time, isn't it? To be walking around on cloud nine, walking around with a smile on my face?

And my spiritual beliefs have changed. Absolutely. Of course now I believe in a life after death. Of course I do. I couldn't not. I believe that I will die but my spirit will live on. I think the object is not to come back here at all, but to go on to another plane. I do believe that. But I believe it takes time to get there. And I know I'm not ready yet. I wish I was but I know I'm not.

And another way it's changed me is that I'm more
understanding toward other people, now I'm much
more understanding about where they're coming from.
I'm much more compassionate and less judgemental.
Not totally, but I try. I really try.

I feel like I'm making progress now, I really do. And
I feel this angel has helped me to know what things are
important. It's so important to grow as a whole person
or as a whole spirit, as a whole being.

I was searching before this happened . . . I know
this'll sound funny . . . but now, somehow, I'm not
searching as much. I guess now I *know* I'll be shown
the way and I'll be helped.

Many other people told me of a feeling of enhanced self-
worth after their angel experience. Beth, the medium, said:

I think once you start to rely on your own angelic
guidance and your own intuition rather than relying on
what other people say, you start to change your self-
worth ideas. You might go through a period when
people will ridicule you for what you're doing, but then
you really have to put it on the line and stand up and
be counted. You know, 'This was my experience. It
might be against all logic but I know it is true.' And
that attitude really starts to bring a strength within.
And I feel that contact with angels or angelic beings
really reinforces that. It really does.

And Margot, a radio broadcaster who saw four angelic beings during childbirth, said:

I feel we have to combat fear because fear is stopping us doing anything. It's stopping us growing as individuals, as communities, as a planet. Even with something like the angels, people are fearful. They'll laugh at it, they'll make fun of it because they're fearful. But if it's happened it's just a fact that it's a part of your life. I'm not fearful of being laughed at or ridiculed and if you're not fearful it gives you such strength.

When it happened I told lots of people, I was so excited by it. In the euphoria. [laughs] You know, 'Guess what happened? I saw the angels!' [laughs] One of my sisters said, 'No, no I don't believe that. I'm sorry.' Some people did say that.

But I'd like to think I was normalising these things by talking about them on radio. And whenever I talk about my angel experience on air people ring up and tell me about theirs.

Another thing this experience did was make me very unafraid of death. It is awesome. When I think about death I think about it as a really beautiful thing. And I'm really looking forward to seeing the angels. Hopefully, I'll see them again here. But if I don't see them now, then I'll certainly see them when I die.

We've moved so far away from the spiritual path. Our lives should be much more open to these sorts of experience, and to the trust and love that come along with them. Not a selfish love but a love and respect for every thing. My sense of all this is that there's something I am supposed to do. But I feel I've just got to be patient. I know eventually, when the time is right, it will be made clear to me where I'm needed.

## What can we learn from the angels?

As we have just seen, we can learn that angels are always there for us, and that we can be secure in their love. We can learn not to fear death and to hand over to them any fear of life we might have. We learn of the need to evolve, to transform ourselves in their image. We gain awareness, openness and inner strength. We learn trust, tolerance, love and compassion. In their very essence angels have much to teach us. The divine attributes they embody include such qualities as peace and inner calm, patience and trust, love and compassion, knowledge and wisdom. And in their every action they exemplify service.

The lesson of patience is a hard one to learn, yet the realisation that it is something worth striving for is mentioned again and again by people who have had angel experiences. And patience is almost always tied in with trust. To be patient we need to trust that everything will happen as it should. We need to trust that when the time is right, the next step will be revealed to us—an opportunity will arise. Perhaps a new door will open, or perhaps a door will close, forcing us in a new direction.

When a door closes, we humans tend to become upset because too often we forget the eternal spiritual truth that an ending *always* signals a new beginning—the moment of death is also the glorious moment of transformation and rebirth. But, even if we do know this, whenever change of any kind is afoot we still need trust, and courage, whether it is to wait patiently for the next spiritual indicator, or to take the first step out into the unknown.

On occasions it becomes obvious that time is not a concept that has any great meaning for angels. Having experienced timelessness myself during my near-death experience, I do understand and appreciate the peace this brings. But, as the earthbound creature I now am, this understanding, although it helps, certainly does not always make it easy to wait upon the angels in everyday life. I, along with everyone else, need patience, trust and courage to weather the tests and frustrations as I am guided along my life's path.

What I have learned is that there is no point in getting worked up about delays and there is certainly no point in trying to force our way through situations. As Lisa said earlier, she learned from Angel Raphael that being in a hurry can be quite counter-productive—if we rush impetuously ahead with our plans we can miss subtle signals and end up running headlong in the wrong direction.

Contact with the angels shows us repeatedly that we do not always know when the time is right for something to happen. I remember, when my shoulders were at their most painful, I wanted them to be healed immediately but I can see now I was not yet ready to move on to the next stage. Had my prayers been answered at that point, my life would have had to take a very different turn. But as it turned out, as frustrated and downhearted as I felt at the time, the angels knew what was best for me. The vision angels have of our lives is so much clearer than our own, and far grander. And as a result of following angelic guidance over the years, my life has been blessed in ways I could never have foreseen, or even dreamed of.

It is often said that we should thank God for the testing times because it is only through the tempering of our souls that we are made ready to do the work of the divine here on earth. But, as important as it is to accept the difficult situations in which we find ourselves from time to time, it is equally important not to become mired in the hardships.

I was often told, 'everything is as it should be', 'this is a time of preparation', 'be steadfast and true' and 'look always to the light'. And I have had many people report similar messages. So, rather than focussing attention only on our misfortunes, allowing ourselves to be drawn further and further into the darkness, we are guided instead to acknowledge the situation, but then to look to the light and ask the angels for help. Once we have asked though, we need then to leave matters in their hands, and trust that everything will be taken care of exactly as it should be. This does not mean there is nothing for us to do. We need to keep the focus on the light by continuing our spiritual practices and doing anything else that can have a positive impact on the situation. The lesson is to do what we *can* but then to hand over to the angels what we cannot handle ourselves, to trust that it will be taken care of; and be grateful. It may well be that it is not the right time either for healing or resolution, but whenever we call on the angels, the very least we can expect is comfort, encouragement, peace and love.

By asking for help and concentrating our awareness and attention on the light in this way, inevitably we not only draw the angels to us but also keep them with us. And as White Eagle teaches, by doing this, we benefit not only ourselves, but all humankind. He says:

You cannot make one effort towards heaven without
the whole of the world, even the very earth itself, being
the better for it.[1]


By swelling the stream of white light on earth we are
playing an important part in tipping the balance away from
the negativity that pollutes so much of our globe.

Many people feel helpless in the face of the many wars,
and the violence and ruthless behaviour, that have charac-
terised and so besmirched life on our planet during the
twentieth century. And they worry that they are not taking
an active enough role in responding to it. But to respond
in kind is not the answer and can only diminish us further.
It is unfortunately obvious that as individuals we cannot
change the sorrowful state of all the suffering lives on this
planet but we can change *our* lives, and *our* attitudes, and
thereby have an effect on the lives of those around us. And
it is urgent that we do so.

Joseph Campbell once said, 'We can't rid the world of
sorrow, but we can choose to live in joy.'[2] This may initially
sound heartless but as we have been told by the angels, joy
is our true nature, and it is therefore through joy that we
connect with the divine core of being. Saint Bonaventure,
the thirteenth century Christian mystic, believed that the
presence of angels in our lives would inevitably open our
eyes to the divine light in every living thing. This he believed
would enable us to truly see the beauty of the world around
us and appreciate the inherently sacred nature of all life. Violence and cruelty would be completely out of place in such
a world. Living in joy therefore can be a profound act of
service. And remember, joy and light, knowledge and

wisdom, compassion and love are the keynotes of the angelic realm. If we were to follow the divine example of angels and live our lives, whatever our occupation, by these principles, we could do no better. As Sogyal Rinpoche writes:

> To transform yourself truly and learn how to be reborn as a transformed being to help others is really to help the world in the most powerful way of all.[3]

# Afterword

Margot said:

I'm the most flawed human being. Why did I see angels? It's just weird. Then I think, 'Well, if it happened to me—I'm no goody-two-shoes—then it's normal and it's for everyone.'

And it is for everyone. Some might find it surprising, but even people who just hear or read about angel experiences can find that their lives begin to change also. I believe this is because they too begin to see the world through different eyes. They too awaken to the presence of the divine in every thing around them. They become more aware of life's daily miracles—the synchronicities and moments of magic that add texture and serendipity to an otherwise unremarkable landscape. They begin to see enchantment where previously they saw only the mundane trappings of everyday life. And *their* priorities also begin to shift.

There is always a mundane side to our earthbound lives but to proclaim this to be the only reality is to limit our horizons unacceptably, and exclude us from a depth of experience and knowledge that is in fact there for the taking. The spiritual realm does exist and to pretend otherwise is a futile exercise. I feel that most people know this in their hearts, and many are eager to embrace the sacred dimension in their lives. But within a culture that sets such store by reason, to suggest that there is *more*, can seem so unreasonable. Yet even some of the twentieth century's greatest physicists have been outspoken about the limitations of physical methods for discovering the true nature of the universe. They have remarked on the mystery at the heart of the physical realm and the inability of Newtonian physics to penetrate its depth. Sir James Jeans wrote:

> Physicists who are trying to understand Nature may work in many different fields and by many different methods; one may dig, one may sow, one may reap. But the final harvest will always be a sheaf of mathematical formulae. These will never describe Nature itself ... [Thus] our studies can never put us into contact with reality.[1]

Quantum mechanics has shown that the whole class of realistic local theories of the universe, including materialism, are untenable. Yet even most scientific life in the west goes on as though quantum mechanics never existed; and its philosophical implications remain largely ignored.

By refusing to acknowledge the mystery at the heart of being, by holding on to 'the known world' as if our lives depended on it, we remain stuck in the material realm and our souls die of malnutrition. On the other hand, by opening ourselves to the numinous, to the sacred and mysterious in life, we may no longer have all the facts, but life becomes enchanting and filled with meaning. As we explore its inner recesses we open ourselves to the music of the spheres, and engage with the harmonics of our souls. Instead of leading a blinkered existence we see the world through the eyes of wonder, we see beauty everywhere around us and, enriched and humbled, we learn to view it with reverence. As Teilhard de Chardin said:

> Some day, after we have mastered the winds, the waves,
> the tides and gravity, ... we shall harness ... the
> energies of love. Then, for the second time in the
> history of the world, man will have discovered fire.[2]

We do not need to see an angel physically standing before us in order to partake of the numinous. On the contrary, by becoming aware of the numinous dimension of *all* things, we find we are forever in the company of angels.

# Endnotes

Introduction
1 Mallasz, *Talking with Angels*, pp.404–405.
2 Plato, *The Republic*, p.320.
3 Moore, *The Re-enchantment of Everyday Life*, p.348.


Chapter 1   What are Angels?
1 Hebrews 13:2.
2 Jung, *Answer to Job*, pp.147–148.
3 Dionysius has often been confused with Dionysius the Areopagite—converted by St Paul—and is sometimes known as Pseudo–Dionysius or Dionysius the Pseudo–Areopagite.
4 All quotations from Dionysius's *Celestial Hierarchies* are taken from Fox & Sheldrake, *The Physics of Angels*, pp.31–55.
5 Margolies, *A Gathering of Angels*, pp.188–189.
6 White Eagle, *Spiritual Unfoldment2*, p.50.
7 Margolies, *A Gathering of Angels*, p.82.
8 Swedenborg in Fox & Rose, *Conversations with Angels*, p.137.

9 White Eagle, *The Quiet Mind*, pp.46–47.

10 Roob, *Alchemy and Mysticism*, p.20.

11 Sutherland, *Children of the Light*, p.90.

12 Lundahl, 'Angels in near-death experiences', pp.51–52.

13 Bunson, *Angels A to Z*, p.181.

14 Davidson, *A Dictionary of Angels*, p.193. 'In Rabbinic lore, this was the size of Adam before he sinned.'

15 Bunson, *Angels A to Z*, p.180.

16 Davidson, *A Dictionary of Angels*, p.193.

17 For further detail see Bunson, *Angels A to Z*, pp.180–181; Davidson, *A Dictionary of Angels*, pp.192–193; Guiley, *Encyclopedia of Angels*, pp.127–128.

18 Swedenborg in Fox & Rose, *Conversations with Angels*, p.60.

19 Davidson, *A Dictionary of Angels*, p.151. In other sources the rank of the Ishim can differ greatly. According to Louis Ginzberg, *The Legends of the Jews II*, p.308, they are thought to be made of fire and ice and reside in the fifth heaven where Moses encountered them. In the *Zohar* they are equated with the ben Elim, the Sons of God mentioned in Genesis 6:2. And according to Pico della Mirandola (fifteenth century) they are ranked ninth. (See Bunson, *Angels A to Z*, p.142; Davidson, *A Dictionary of Angels*, p.151.)

20 Morse, *Parting Visions*, p.14.

21 Genesis 18:1–15.

22 Genesis 19:1–25.

23 Tobit 11:13.

24 Maclean, *To Hear the Angels Sing*, pp.191–192. The term 'deva' is a Sanskrit word meaning shining one. Devas, according to Dorothy Maclean's experience 'hold the archetypal pattern and plan for all forms around us,

and they direct the energy needed for materializing them'. (p.58) When contacting, for example, the pea deva, contact is not made with one particular deva but rather with the essence of *all* pea devas. For more detail see Maclean, *The Findhorn Garden*, pp.53–99.

25  Howard, *Commune with the Angels*, p.30. For more detail see Isaac, *Flower Newhouse's Angels of Nature*, pp.101–111.

26  Isaac, *Flower Newhouse's Angels of Nature*, p.45.

27  Isaac, *Flower Newhouse's Angels of Nature*, p.34.

28  White Eagle, *Spiritual Unfoldment2*, p.93.

29  Jung, *Answer to Job*, p.xiv.

30  Campbell, *The Power of Myth*, pp.217–218.

31  The whole world is a circle, says Joseph Campbell. This is a view that has been shared by many throughout time, and often taken literally. For instance, in a work by A. Cellarius, produced in 1660, the 'superlunary world' or 'ethereal heavens' is depicted as a series of concentric circles or spheres that move within each other with the earth fixed at their centre. Alexander Roob (*Alchemy and Mysticism*, p.51) notes that 'the outermost, opaque sphere of the fixed stars was known as the *Primum Mobile*, the 'first moved', because, driven by divine love, it caused the motion of all other spheres. This *Primum Mobile* was seen to be God Himself, embracing all others and setting in motion the 'music of the spheres', a system of perfect harmony. Roob (p.96) further quotes A. Kircher who wrote in 1650, 'from the earth to the starry heavens is a perfect octave'.

32  For more detail see Campbell, *The Power of Myth*, pp.214–217.

33  Jung, *Mandala Symbolism*, p.41. In addition, the point

within the circle symbolises the unity of the microcosm and macrocosm. Roob (*Alchemy and Mysticism*, p.329) notes that in 1604 Rosicrucian Theophilius Schweighart drew a diagram in which the connection between microcosm and macrocosm was to be contemplated: *Omnia ab uno* (Everything from the One), *Omnia ad uno* (Everything to the One). He wrote, 'Seriously contemplate nature, and then the elements ... therein you will finally rediscover yourself, from which you then ascend to God Almighty'.

34 In addition, in alchemy, the mandala is to be found in the *quadratura circuli* which, according to Jung (*Mandala Symbolism*, p.3), represents the 'synthesis of the four elements which are forever tending to fall apart'.

35 Jung, *Mandala Symbolism*, p.6.

36 Guiley and Place, *The Angels Tarot*, pp.47–49.


Chapter 2   What do Angels really look like?

1 Lewis & Oliver, *Angels A to Z*, p.221.

2 See video—'Entertaining Angels Unawares'. Carlton UK Productions in association with Pascavision Ltd.

3 Guiley, *Encyclopedia of Angels*, p.165.

4 Morse, *Closer to the Light*, p.33.

5 Sutherland, *Within the Light*, pp.228–229.

6 Serdahely, 'The near-death experience: Is the presence always the higher self?', p.133.

7 Isaac, *Flower Newhouse's Angels of Nature*, p.6.

8 Moody, *The Light Beyond*, p.10.

9 St Teresa of Avila, *The Life of Saint Teresa of Avila by Herself*, p.210.

10 Sutherland, *Beloved Visitors*, p.195.

11 See Peter Paul Rubens, 'Madonna in a Garland of Flowers' (c.1616).

12 See Mentré, *Illuminated Manuscripts of Medieval Spain*; and Grubb, *Revelations: Art of the Apocalypse*, pp.34–35.

13 Mozarabic painting was a distinctive form of Christian art that emerged in Spain between the eighth and eleventh centuries, its greatest flowering occurring during the tenth century. It drew on the diverse religious artistic traditions that were centred in, or passed through, the Iberian Peninsula during that period—Judaic, Islamic, Byzantine, Coptic and even Ethiopian. The genius of the Mozarabic painters lay in their ability to draw together these diverse influences and create a truly original body of work, unique in the medieval world. (See Mentré, *Illuminated Manuscripts of Medieval Spain*).

14 'The Fifth Trumpet', from Lambertus, *Liber Floridus*, in Grubb, *Revelations: Art of the Apocalypse*, p.27.

15 Even in the Bible, little distinction seems to be made between God and the Angel of the Lord, his representative on earth. As already noted, Metatron, as the Angel of the Lord, takes his place at the top of the Tree of Life, and as the Angel of the Face is the outward manifestation of an in-dwelling God. For instance, in Exodus 23:20, God promises that an angel will be sent to guard and lead the people out, but warns that they must pay attention and 'obey his voice' since 'my name is in him'.

16 See Davidson, *A Dictionary of Angels*, pp.193–195.

17 The Koran is the sacred book of Islam and is conventionally divided into *suras* or chapters. It is believed to be the direct word of God and was received by the

Prophet Mohammed in a series of revelations.
18 See Wilson, *Angels: Messengers of the Gods*, p.41.
19 Kerubim had the bodies of sphinxes or bulls and the heads of humans.
20 See Wilson, *Angels: Messengers of the Gods*, pp.6–7.
21 See Wilson, *Angels: Messengers of the Gods*, p.37.
22 See Wilson, *Angels: Messengers of the Gods*, p.74.
23 Grubb, *Angels*, pp.13–14.
24 See Wilson, *Angels: Messengers of the Gods*, pp.82–85.
25 See Wilson, *Angels: Messengers of the Gods*, p.36.
26 Neihardt, *Black Elk Speaks*, p.40.
27 For more information about Isis see Walker, *The Woman's Encyclopaedia of Myths and Secrets*, pp.453–456.
28 Founded by Iranian prophet Zoroaster c.1400 BC.
29 Wilson, *Angels: Messengers of the Gods*, p.44.
30 Barrett, *Death-Bed Visions*, p.62.
31 Ring, 'Amazing Grace: The near-death experience as a compensatory gift', p.15.
32 Hoffman, *Visions of Innocence*, p.9.
33 Whitfield, 'Interview with Boyd Salter', p.35.

Chapter 3  How do we meet Angels?
1 Moore, *The Re-Enchantment of Everyday Life*, pp.172–180.
2 Kirven, *Angels in Action*, pp.13–14.
3 Maclean, *To Hear the Angels Sing*, pp.121–122.
4 Maclean, *To Hear the Angels Sing*, p.151.
5 Maclean, *To Hear the Angels Sing*, p.152.
6 Harner, *The Way of the Shaman*, pp.11–13.
7 Harner, *The Way of the Shaman*, p.20.

8 Scientists curious about why drums are used in so many cultures around the world have found that a monotonous drumbeat actually changes brainwaves from their usual *beta* state to a *theta* range (similar to a state of very deep meditation).

9 See Neihardt, *Black Elk Speaks*, pp.26–43.

10 That state of confusion and helplessness also indicates to me that they are suffering, in shamanic terms, a loss of power and probably even loss of soul, both of which can be retrieved from non-ordinary reality to bring about a healing.

Chapter 4    Angel timing

1 Hoffman, *Visions of Innocence*, pp.156–157.

2 Morse, *Parting Visions*, pp. 21–22.

3 Oski, F.A. 'An Epiphany?' *Contemporary Pediatrics* 10 (1993):9–10 (Referenced in Morse, *Parting Visions*, bibliography).

4 Eason, *Psychic Power of Children*, pp.128–129.

5 Hoffman, *Visions of Innocence*, p.70.

6 Gallup, *Adventures in Immortality*, pp.94–95.

7 Hoffman, *Visions of Innocence*, p.72.

8 Sutherland, *Transformed by the Light*.

9 Morse et al., 'Childhood near–death experiences', p.1112.

10 Gallup, *Adventures in Immortality*, pp.91–92.

11 Margolies, *A Gathering of Angels*, p.189.

12 Mallasz, *Talking with Angels*, p.405.

13 Zaleski, *Otherworld Journeys*, p.24.

14 See Morse, *Closer to the Light*, pp.128–130.

15 Serdahely, 'Pediatric near-death experiences', p.35.

16 See Moody, *The Light Beyond*, pp.45–59.

17 See Ring, *Heading Toward Omega*, pp.64–66.
18 See Morse, *Closer to the Light*, p.35.
19 Zaleski, *Otherworld Journeys*, p.58.
20 See Neihardt, *Black Elk Speaks*, pp.27–43.
21 Barrett, *Death-Bed Visions*, p.11.
22 Barrett, *Death-Bed Visions*, p.61.
23 Barrett, *Death-Bed Visions*, p.102.
24 Osis & Haraldsson, *At the Hour of Death*, p.88.
25 Osis & Haraldsson, *At the Hour of Death*, p.93.
26 In Osis & Haraldsson's study, the sample of dying patients who saw apparitions comprised 216 American cases and 233 Indian cases (p.90).
27 Osis & Haraldsson, *At the Hour of Death*, p.92.
28 Osis & Haraldsson, *At the Hour of Death*, p.113.
29 1 Chronicles 21:14–16.
30 Bunson, *Angels A–Z*, p.73.
31 Bunson, *Angels A–Z*, p.34.
32 Kabbani, *Angels Unveiled: A Sufi Perspective*, p.208.
33 Sutherland, *Children of the Light*, p.90.
34 Kabbani, *Angels Unveiled: A Sufi Perspective*, pp.210–211.
35 Lewis & Oliver, *Angels A to Z*, p.19.
36 See Wilson, *Angels: Messengers of the Gods*, p.55.
37 Kabbani, *Angels Unveiled: A Sufi Perspective*, p.213.
38 See Kabbani, *Angels Unveiled: A Sufi Perspective*, pp.108–109.
39 White Eagle, *Spiritual Unfoldment2*, pp.57–58.


Chapter 5   Angel roles
1 See Ring, *Heading Toward Omega*, pp.76–81.
2 Serdahely, 'Loving help from the other side', p.180.

3 See William's story in Sutherland, *Beloved Visitors*, pp.190–203.
4 See Howard, *Commune with the Angels*, pp.41–45.
5 Howard, *Commune with the Angels*, p.44.
6 See Ring, *Heading Toward Omega*, pp.61–63.
7 Ring, *Heading Toward Omega*, p.67.
8 Ring, *Heading Toward Omega*, p.71.
9 See Shana's story in Sutherland, *Within the Light*, pp.261–268.
10 See Margolies, *A Gathering of Angels*, pp.194–195.
11 See Giovetti, *Angels: The Role of Celestial Guardians and Beings of Light*, pp.244–247.
12 See Ring, 'Amazing Grace: The near-death experience as a compensatory gift', pp.14–17.
13 Jung, *Memories, Dreams, Reflections*, pp.320–329.
14 See Ring, 'Amazing Grace: The near-death experience as a compensatory gift', pp.28–33.
15 See Hal's story in Sutherland, *Children of the Light*, pp.166–187.
16 Rinpoche, *The Tibetan Book of Living and Dying*, p.330.
17 See Carol Zaleski's remarkable book, *Otherworld Journeys*, for a detailed examination of medieval NDE accounts.
18 Bede, *A History of the English Church and People*, p.421.
19 Zaleski, *Otherworld Journeys*, p.32.
20 See Bede, *A History of the English Church and People*, pp.420–421.
21 Zaleski, *Otherworld Journeys*, p.32.
22 See Zaleski, *Otherworld Journeys*, p.77.
23 Zaleski, *Otherworld Journeys*, p.69.

24  See Zaleski, *Otherworld Journeys*, pp.29–30.
25  Margolies, *A Gathering of Angels*, p.10.
26  See Lewis & Oliver, *Angels A to Z*, pp.209–210.
27  Jovanovic, *An Inquiry into the Existence of Guardian Angels*, pp. 151–152.
28  A bodhisattva is a saviour figure who delays his/her own spiritual enlightenment in order to continue helping other, lesser, beings.
29  Davis, *Myths and Legends of Japan*, pp.106–107.
30  Lewis & Oliver, *Angels A to Z*, p.196.
31  Lewis & Oliver, *Angels A to Z*, pp.186–194.
32  Lundahl, *Collection of Near-Death Research Readings*, pp.170–171.
33  Zaleski, *Otherworld Journeys*, p.54.
34  Moody, *Reflections on Life After Life*, pp.24–25.
35  Zaleski, *Otherworld Journeys*, p.29.
36  Serdahely, 'Loving Help from the Other Side', p.175.
37  See Burnham, *A Book of Angels*, pp. 72–74.
38  Jovanovic, *An Inquiry into the Existence of Guardian Angels*, p.5.
39  Jovanovic, *An Inquiry into the Existence of Guardian Angels*, p.108.
40  *Evening Standard*, 27 December 1997.
41  Burnham, *A Book of Angels*, pp.26–27.
42  See video—'Entertaining Angels Unawares'. Carlton UK Productions in association with Pascavision Ltd.
43  Mallasz, *Talking with Angels*, p.397.

Chapter 6   Living in the company of Angels
1  White Eagle, *The Quiet Mind*, p.53.
2  Campbell in Osbon, *A Joseph Campbell Companion*, p.193.

3 Rinpoche, *The Tibetan Book of Living and Dying*, p.364.

Afterword
1 Wilber, *Quantum Questions*, p.8.
2 In Rinpoche, *The Tibetan Book of Living and Dying*, p.364.

Grateful acknowledgement is made to the following publishers for the permission to reproduce extracts used in this book. All attempts have been made, where possible, to locate the appropriate copyright holders.

Campbell, J with Moyers, B. *The Power of the Myth* (1988)—Doubleday (US)
Jovanovic, P. *An Inquiry into the Existence of Guardian Angels* (1995)—M.E. Evans & Co Inc. (US)
Jung, C.J. *Mandala Symbolism* (1973)—Princeton University Press (US)
Moore, T. *The Re-Enchantment of Everyday Life* (1996)—Hodder & Stoughton
Rinpoche. *The Tibetan Book of Living and Dying* (1992)—Rider (UK)

# Bibliography

Barrett, W. (1986). *Death-Bed Visions*. Aquarian, North-amptonshire. (First published in 1926.)

Bede, (1968). *A History of the English Church and People*. (Translated by Leo Sherley-Price), Penguin Books, Harmondsworth.

*The HarperCollins Study Bible* (New Revised Standard Version). (1989). HarperCollins Publishers, New York.

Bunson, M. (1996). *Angels A to Z*. Crown Trade Paperbacks, New York.

Burnham, S. (1990). *A Book of Angels*. Ballantine Books, New York.

Campbell, J. with Moyers, B. (1988). *The Power of Myth*. Doubleday, New York.

Colgrave, B. & Mynors, R.A.B. (eds.) (1969). *Bede's Ecclesiastical History of the English People*. Oxford University Press, London.

Davidson, G. (1971). *A Dictionary of Angels*. The Free Press, A Division of Macmillan, New York.

Davis, F.H. (1989). *Myths and Legends of Japan*. Graham Brash (Pte) Ltd. Singapore.

Eason, C. (1994). *Psychic Power of Children*. Foulsham, London.
'Entertaining Angels Unawares', Carlton UK Productions in association with Pascavision Ltd.

Fox, L. & Rose, D.L. (eds.) (1996). *Conversation with Angels: What Swedenborg Heard in Heaven*. Chrysalis Books, West Chester, Pennsylvania.
Fox, M. & Sheldrake, R. (1996). *The Physics of Angels*. HarperCollins, San Francisco.

Gallup, G. Jr. (1983). *Adventures in Immortality*. Souvenir Press, London.
Ginzberg, L. (1954), *The Legends of the Jews*. (7 volumes). The Jewish Publication Society of America, Philadelphia.
Giovetti, P. (1993). *Angels: The Role of Celestial Guardians and Beings of Light*. Samuel Weiser, Inc., York Beach, ME.
Grubb, N. (1995). *Angels*. A Tiny Folio, Abbeville Press Publishers, New York.
Grubb, N. (1997). *Revelations: Art of the Apocalypse*. Abbeville Press Publishers, New York.
Guiley, R.E. & Place, R.M. (1995). *The Angels' Tarot*. HarperCollins, New York.
Guiley, R.E. (1996). *Encyclopedia of Angels*. Facts on File, New York.

Harner, M. (1990). *The Way of the Shaman*. Harper San Francisco, New York. (Third Edition)

Hoffman, E. (1992). *Visions of Innocence*. Shambhala, Boston & New York.

Howard, J. (1992). *Commune with the Angels*. A.R.E. Press, Virginia Beach, Virginia.

Isaac, S. (ed.) (1995). *Flower A. Newhouse's Angels of Nature*. Quest Books, Wheaton IL.

Jovanovic, P. (1995). *An Inquiry into the Existence of Guardian Angels*. M.Evans and Company, Inc., New York.

Jung, C.G. (1973). *Mandala Symbolism*. Bollingen Series, Princeton University Press, Princeton NJ. (First published 1959.)

Jung, C.G. (1979). *Answer to Job*. Routledge & Kegan Paul, London. (First published 1952.)

Jung, C.G. (1995). *Memories, Dreams, Reflections*. Fontana Press, London. (First published 1961.)

Kabbani, S.M.H. (1995). *Angels Unveiled: A Sufi Perspective*. Kazi Publications, Inc., Chicago IL.

Kirven, R.H. (1994). *Angels in Action: What Swedenborg Saw and Heard*. Chrysalis Books, West Chester, Pennsylvania.

Lewis, J.R. & Oliver, E.D. (1996). *Angels A to Z*. Visible Ink Press, Detroit.

Lundahl, C. (1982). 'Near-death experiences of Mormons' in Lundahl, C. (ed.). *A Collection of Near-Death Research Readings*. Nelson-Hall, Chicago.

Lundahl, C. (1992). 'Angels in near-death experiences', *Journal of Near-Death Studies*, Vol.11, No.1, pp.49–56.

Maclean, D. in The Findhorn Community. (1975). *The Findhorn Garden*. Turnstone Books/Wildwood House Publishers, London.

Maclean, D. (1990). *To Hear the Angels Sing*. Lindisfarne Press, New York. (First published 1980.)

Mallasz, G. (1988). *Talking with Angels*. Daimon Verlag, Einsiedeln. [This document from Hungary is transcribed by Gitta Mallasz, English rendition by Robert Hinshaw, assisted by Gitta Mallasz and Lela Fischli.]

Margolies, M.B. (1994). *A Gathering of Angels*. Ballantine Books, New York.

Mentré, M. (1996). *Illuminated Manuscripts of Medieval Spain*. Thames & Hudson, London.

Moody, R.A. Jr. (1978). *Reflections on Life After Life*. Bantam Books, New York.

Moody, R.A. Jr. (1988). *The Light Beyond*. Bantam Books, New York.

Moore, T. (1996). *The Re-enchantment of Everyday Life*. A Hodder & Stoughton Book, Hodder Headline, Australia.

Morse, M. with Perry, P. (1990). *Closer to the Light*. Villard Books, New York.

Morse, M. with Perry, P. (1994). *Parting Visions*. Judy Piatkus (Publishers) Ltd., London.

Morse, M. (1983). 'A near-death experience in a 7-year-old child', *American Journal of Diseases of Children*, Vol.137, No.10, pp.959–961.

Morse, M., Castillo, P., Venecia, D. et al. (1986). 'Childhood Near-Death Experiences', *American Journal of Diseases of Children*, Vol.140, No.11, pp.1110–1114.

Neihardt, J.G. (1974). *Black Elk Speaks*. Abacus edition published by Sphere Books, London.

Osbon, D.K. (ed.) (1991). *A Joseph Campbell Companion: Reflections on the Art of Living*. HarperCollins Publishers, New York.

Osis, K. & Haraldsson, E. (1990 Revised edition). *At the Hour of Death*. Hastings House Book Publishers, New York.

Plato. (1987). *The Republic*. Penguin Books, Harmondsworth.

Ring, K. (1984). *Heading Toward Omega*. Quill, William Morrow, New York.

Ring, K. (1991). 'Amazing Grace: The near-death experience as a compensatory gift', *Journal of Near-Death Studies*, Vol.10, No.1, pp.11–39.

Rinpoche, S. (1992). *The Tibetan Book of Living and Dying*. Rider Books, London.

Roob, A. (1997). *Alchemy and Mysticism*. Taschen, Köln.

St. Teresa of Avila. (1987). *The Life of St. Teresa of Avila by Herself*. (J.M. Cohen trans.) Penguin Books, London.

Serdahely, W. (1987). 'The near-death experience: Is the presence always the higher self?', *Omega*, Vol.18, No.2, pp.129–134.

Serdahely, W. (1990). 'Pediatric near-death experiences', *Journal of Near-Death Studies*, Vol.9, No.1, pp.33–39.

Serdahely, W. (1992). 'Loving help from the other side: A mosaic of some near-death, and near-death-like experiences', *Journal of Near-Death Studies*, Vol.10, No.3, pp.171–182.

Sutherland, C. (1992). *Transformed by the Light*. Bantam Books, Sydney.

Sutherland, C. (1993). *Within the Light*. Bantam Books, Sydney.

Sutherland, C. (1995). *Children of the Light*. Bantam Books, Sydney.

Sutherland, C. (1997). *Beloved Visitors*. Bantam Books, Sydney.

Walker, B.G. (1995). *The Woman's Encyclopedia of Myths and Secrets*. Pandora, Hammersmith, London. (First published by HarperCollins 1993).

White Eagle. (1987). *The Quiet Mind*. The White Eagle Publishing Trust, Liss, Hampshire. (First published 1972).

White Eagle. (1989). *Spiritual Unfoldment2: The Ministry of Angels and the Invisible World of Nature*. The White Eagle Publishing Trust, Liss, Hampshire. (First published 1969).

Whitfield, R. (1995). 'Interview with Boyd Salter', *On Eagles' Wings*, Vol.3, No.1, p.35.

Wilber, K. (ed.) (1984). *Quantum Questions: Mystical Writings of the World's Greatest Physicists*. Shambhala Publications, Boulder, Colorado.

Wilson, P.L. (1994). *Angels: Messengers of the Gods*. Thames & Hudson, London.

Zaleski, C. (1988). *Otherworld Journeys*. Oxford University Press, New York.

# *Index*